I'm Not a Millionaire, but I'm Debt Free:

Depression-and-recession-proof Living

Table of Contents

Chapter One

The Step before the First Step

I am not a millionaire, but I am debt free. This is the truth: my wife and I are young adults (at least, we think we are still young), and we own our home; there is no mortgage. We own our car; there is no loan. We own our appliances and furniture; there is nothing under lease. We have zero credit card debt, and we don't owe anyone money. We, on top of all this, are blessed to have every necessity of life.

We did not arrive at this point in life because we are extraordinary people. Neither of us attended an Ivy League University; although, we are happy for those who did and who can. Neither of us was *born* into money; it's fair to state we were both raised in lower-class households. Also, we did not arrive at this point by our involvement in a get-rich-quick scheme, by gambling or playing the lottery. Simply put: I have worked at a middle-sized church in Kansas City, Missouri for the past several years, and my wife has homeschooled our children.

Furthermore, I did not cultivate a ground-breaking invention. I have never been a savvy real-estate entrepreneur. I did not get here because of world-class athletic ability like so many young boys dream to have. I could never throw a football forty yards on a line, score a basketball at will in the low post, or turn on a ninety-eight mile-per-hour fastball and drive it four-hundred feet. There are some who can, and, again, I am happy for them. This was never me. I was not at the top of my small-college class, and I was not even at the top of my high-school class.

On one hand, I feel disqualified from writing this book. The reason: by most standards, I have nothing extraordinary to offer. I am a man of average height, average build, and, according to standardized testing, average intelligence. However, when I read such an *average* description of myself, it leads me to change my mind. Instead, I believe I am exactly the person to write this book. Most people weren't *born* into money, either. Most people didn't graduate from an Ivy League institution, either. Most people can't turn on a major-league fastball, either. Millions come from middle-to-lower-class households, bringing me to the following, wonderful conclusion: if I did it, anyone can do it.

Therefore, it is my pleasure to share with you exactly how I arrived at this point in my life. I am not going to withhold anything essential from you. If it is written in this book, it played a role in getting me to this point. I will give you the truth. Yes, the truth can be difficult; however, the truth will never fail you.

I am not the foremost authority on the subject of money. This book is not the foremost authority on the subject of money. The Bible, the Word of God, is the foremost authority on all subjects, including money.

My son, give attention to my words;

Incline your ear to my sayings.

Do not let them depart from your eyes;

Keep them in the midst of your heart;

For they are life to those who find them,

And health to all their flesh.

Proverbs 4:20-22

I share all of the information in this book without a particle of boasting in me. Rather, I give all credit to the reason for my accomplishment.

That, as it is written, "He who glories, let him glory in the Lord."

1 Corinthians 1:31

God, Jesus, and the Holy Ghost, all three in one, are and is the reason for every accomplishment in my life, including every financial accomplishment. Furthermore, the information in this book has applicable power, and here is ostensible proof of that applicable power. I will explain in detail later in this book that this is not my first occasion to be financially debt free. Instead, I have been debt-free twice. I was debt free ten years ago, but I subsequently made mistakes that placed me, my wife, and our innocent children under the cruel weight of debt again. However, I gladly and humbly present myself before you as debt free again, and this is good news for you. Why is this good news for you? If God rescued me from debt twice, He can surely rescue you from debt once.

What have I done to ascend the mountain of debt-freedom twice? I have believed, confessed, and applied the Word of God. That is it! Fox example, the words I shared a few moments ago in the book of Proverbs: I have believed those words, confessed those words, and applied those words. Not just those words, but as many precious and powerful words from the Word of God as I possibly could.

Here is the step before the first step: faith in God. I could give you several other applicable strategies for financial profusion. However, if I fail to give you the initial step, which is faith in God, I would cause you to misstep right out of the gate. What good would that do? What a setback! To trip at the beginning of the race! To trip and maybe even head in the wrong direction!

I hear and come across many people who are extremely intelligent and well-learned. Even so, their capacity to discuss many issues is ultimately flawed because they are fundamentally incorrect. In short, they missed the key step in forming their opinion, thus the accuracy of their discourse is pushed off course. Let me state it again: the initial step to my financial success has been faith in God; not *was*, but *has been*...because I am still growing and learning from Him each day.

I realize I have already disappointed some of you. Some of you work ardently to avoid God and even conversation about God at all cost. Therefore, admitting you need God to proceed any further is an insult to you, but it is the truth. We must get to the point where truth is most important. Furthermore, accepting truth is not accepting defeat. Instead, accepting truth points us to deliverance, healing, salvation, and victory. Furthermore, truth applies to every area of our lives, including the area of money. Therefore, truth will cause your financial position to experience deliverance, healing, salvation, and victory, as well.

Jesus said to him, "I am the way, the truth, and the life. No one comes to the Father except through Me."

John 14:6

In the beginning was the Word, and the Word was with God, and the Word was God.

John 1:1

"And you shall know the truth, and the truth shall make you free."

John 8:32

Jesus is the Word of God. Jesus is the Bible. Jesus is truth. Thus, when we receive and apply truth, when we receive and apply the teaching of the Word of God, we will know success in every area. Trust me: Jesus brings success and success in every area.

Beloved, I pray that you may prosper in all things and be in health, just as your soul prospers.

3 John, verse 2

God desires for every area of your life to prosper, including the area of your money.

The good news continues. If you already have faith in God, and if you are willing to believe, confess, and apply His Word to the handling of your money, you are well on your way to financial success. Congratulations! On the other hand, even if you have never had faith in God, if you will begin to believe, confess, and apply the Word of God by faith to the handling of your money, first trusting Him before seeing any results, you are on your way to financial success, as well. More importantly, you are on your way to the greatest success possible: salvation from sin and death.

For "whoever calls on the name of the Lord shall be saved."

Romans 10:13

Here are some thoughts as we begin our journey together. I will present many biblical principles in this book. These principles are truth. If you have difficulty accepting the Bible as truth, I recommend you read some specific chapters in my previous books in which I address the scientific, archeological, and historical truth of the Bible. I am not going to take much time in this book to convince anyone the Bible is truth. First and foremost, I cannot convince anyone; the Holy Spirit does the convincing. The Holy Spirt convinced me. Instead, I will explain what God has done in my life. Proving the existence and truth of God is impossible since God is only received by faith.

But without faith it is impossible to please Him, for he who comes to God must believe that He is, and that He is a rewarder of those who diligently seek Him.

Hebrews 11:6

You can keep looking, but you won't see God. However, if you ask God to open your heart, you will see the evidence of God all around you, and He wants to produce His evidence through you as well if you are willing. Again, maybe you are not interested in the Bible. However, if you are interested in truth, you will become interested in the Bible. Some of the subsequent principles will pertain directly to money, and some will have broader application. Again, this is how I arrived at this point in my life, so what else can I share other than what I know?

Intermittently in this book, I will share my personal account with you, explaining how I twice became debt free by the grace of God. I realize you might become frustrated with me as you read this book. You might desire for me to move quickly, addressing the pressing financial issues facing you at this moment: lack of income, budgeting, debt, lack of savings, and etc. You might even face the urge to overextend and scour upcoming sections of this book sooner than later, looking for those topics most pertinent to your financial situation. I encourage you: resist the urge. The best action I will take to assist many of you with your financial matters is this: I will make you slow down. I will make you contemplate. I will make you consider. I will make you process. There is a necessary foundation to be laid. I know the following analogies seem oversimplified, but the penthouse is not built without the ground floor, and the final rock at the top of the mountain is nothing without the first rock at the bottom.

Furthermore, let us be honest with one another: bolting through life with a salvo of hasty financial decisions has brought many of you to this point. It is difficult to accept, but many of you have not been well-served by your choices so far, and neither was I for many years. It is time to try a different way and walk a different road. I am not condemning you or judging you. How could I? I have been there. I have been there, and I have returned from that lifestyle to encourage you that there is an answer for you. Please, take your time and let God reveal the answers to the financial questions confronting you. Again, why do we consult God and His Word? The Word of God is the foremost authority on all subjects, including the area of money.

I write the following blessing over you as you read this book, that God, by His mercy, will soften your heart toward Him. I pray you will read this book in the exact season He desires you to read it, and you will extract from this book exactly what He desires you to extract—nothing more, nothing less. I pray all of your attention be rerouted to Him; He deserves all honor, credit, tribute, and glory for every good and perfect gift. I write this blessing over you, that God, my Heavenly Father, will become everything to you. Furthermore, as you make Him everything, He will take the place of everything in your life that is bad, He will take the place of everything in your life that is wrong, and He will even take the place of everything in your life that is unjust. I write this in the name of Jesus, the Son of God. So be it.

Chapter Two

My Story: How It Started for Me

A little town north of Kansas City, Missouri is where it started for me. I had wonderful parents; awesome parents. I didn't have perfect parents, but I had godly parents. They did not drive me, but they led me. They didn't have much, but they had the joy of the Lord, and I can attest there was a presence of peace in our home. I have a vivid memory of one particular moment in our little kitchen when I encountered the peaceful presence of God for the first time. Other children were raised in wealthier homes than I was raised, but I watched as many of those homes unfortunately unraveled through the years.

There are certain valuables money cannot buy, and we had them. Again, my parents were not perfect, and I was not perfect. They made many mistakes, and I made many mistakes. However, instead of allowing those mistakes to go unchecked and run rampant, we would repent to God and ask for wisdom to live better.

As I reflect, we didn't have much, but we had what we needed. My father worked at a cement-manufacturing plant, and my mother cleaned houses for many years. When I turned five, we moved closer to the city and closer to Dad's job. Their jobs didn't pay much, but I never remember going hungry for a single night. They both served God, and God was faithful. I remember going to work with my mom in the summer while school was on break. She cleaned big, beautiful homes in affluent neighborhoods; two houses per day at twenty-five dollars per house. Somehow, my parents made it work; my father umpired little league baseball and church softball games in the summer for extra money, as well.

Yes, their diligent work-effort was very evident; however, there was another factor that propelled them through life. My parents gave to the Lord.

Jesus said,

"Give, and it will be given to you: good measure, pressed down, shaken together, and running over will be put into your bosom. For with the same measure that you use, it will be measured back to you."

Luke 6:38

Many people master the importance of hard work, but they neglect the essential component of giving. In fact, many people work feverishly until they cross the threshold of overworking. Still, they fail to achieve positive results.

Again, I cannot stress it enough: my parents were godly parents, but they were not perfect parents; they were not perfect, but they were faithful. They honored God, and they honored God by honoring His Word, which meant they gave to the House of the Lord and others. Consequently, God blessed our home with food, clothing, transportation, and the necessities of life. As I reflect, God was not only faithful to bless them, but He was faithful to bless their children because the choices of parents have a direct impact on their seed. The presence of God in our home led me to accept Jesus as savior when I was five. Fast-forward many years, and, ironically, this is roughly the age when both of my children accepted Jesus as savior, as well.

I was a teenager when I remember my mother hearing about a custodial position at a local college. A woman of prayer, she sensed a convincing nudge to seek more information and eventually apply for the job; the idea of stable hours and benefits sounded great to her. All credit to God: she got the job. After she took the job, she discovered another reason why God had lovingly nudged her in that direction—you will find in life that God is better to you than you are to yourself. The college informed her that once she worked there for an entire year, her children would be eligible for tuition remission. In other words, her children would be able to attend college for free. I ask you, how does a family with the father working at a cement plant and the mother working as a custodian get the opportunity to put their children through college for free?

"For with God nothing will be impossible."

Luke 1:37

God had initiated a process far beyond my parents' or my comprehension, and the blessings did not stop there. There was something else that happened while my mother worked at that college. A truck from a local bakery would arrive on campus once per week, possibly delivering to the college cafeteria—I don't remember exactly why. However, there was more behind the purpose of that truck for us. Again, I don't recall all the details, but the remaining contents of that truck were made available to the college custodians. We called the truck "the break truck" in our home. It was full of breads, pastries, and other items—high-end items—that we would never buy at the store. Faithfully, the bread truck would pull on campus once per week...for years. My parents and I would marvel each week at what Mom would bring home; she was giddy to say the least. It seemed she would bring home twenty dollars in bread-truck extras each week, which was a significant amount of grocery money for us at that time. One day, I put some numbers to the items from the bread truck. Twenty dollars per week per year for five years: how does over $5,000 in extra groceries sound? Better yet, based on inflation calculations, our $5,000 in extra groceries then would be the approximate equivalent of $10,750 today. Thus, let me update my question: how does $10,750 in extra groceries sound?

These were just some of the tools God used to bless us and keep us. Furthermore, I watched as my mother saved enough money to pay off our home and add a two-car garage with a driveway while I was still a teenager. I would be hard pressed to find many savvy financial experts who could have accomplished all that she accomplished with what she had. However, to be fair, my mother had an unfair advantage over most *financial experts*. My mother had supernatural help.

God is our refuge and strength,

A very present help in trouble.

Psalm 46:1

As I turned eighteen and began to experience life as an adult, my upbringing and decision-making ability were quickly put to the test—to be continued.

Chapter Three

Money Is a Spiritual Issue First

A primary purpose and recurring theme of this book is to demonstrate that money is a spiritual issue before it is a physical issue. Money, the earning, managing, and investing thereof, begins on a spiritual level before physical results come to pass.

I will readily admit: many others are much more qualified than I am to recommend investment tips, retirement options, scrupulous banking methods, and etc. My expertise is not in those areas. Rather, my goal is to help you pour an infallible foundation on which you can build. Once this foundation is laid, you will be ready to apply all the financial intricacies you desire. However, if not for a dependable foundation molded by concrete precepts, the next financial level will be ever-elusive to you.

Also, I refuse to try to dazzle you with materialistic fallacies or get-rich-quick schemes. Instead, I will share with you two premises I have learned and lived to be true regarding money:

1) If God can bless me, He can bless you.

2) Money (the earning, managing, and investing thereof) begins on a spiritual level before physical results come to pass.

Once we prioritize and master the spiritual behavior of the heart, we then proceed to enjoy the physical benefits wealth provides. It would be of zero benefit to us to hurtle full speed ahead, all the while making radical financial decisions, all the while acting with blatant disregard for the truth: money (the earning, managing, and investing thereof) begins on a spiritual level before physical results come to pass. You can show me two individuals, each with a million dollars, and I can show you two drastically different outcomes.

Money is neutral. How money is used is inevitable. It all begins with the issues of the heart.

Keep your heart with all diligence,

For out of it spring the issues of life.

Proverbs 4:23

Once we understand how to spiritually perceive money, we can then cross all the necessary bridges along the way: how much do we give God, how much do we give others, how do we budget, how do we save, how do we approach debt, how do we invest, and etc. Nevertheless, it is essential to start at the beginning while not missing a step, which is why we must have wisdom.

To know wisdom and instruction,

To perceive the words of understanding,

To receive the instruction of wisdom,

Justice, judgment, and equity;

To give prudence to the simple,

To the young man knowledge and discretion—

A wise man will hear and increase learning,

And a man of understanding will attain wise counsel,

To understand a proverb and an enigma,

The words of the wise and their riddles.

The fear of the Lord is the beginning of knowledge,

But fools despise wisdom and instruction.

Proverbs 1:2-7

As I wrote earlier, I know you are ready to plunge face first in the dollars and cents conversation, and, believe me, we will get there. Even so, we must understand the foundational principles for earning, managing, and investing money before more money finds our hand. If everyone would take time to understand the foundational issues of money before rushing the use of money, more people would benefit, and less people would suffer such cruel consequences.

Money is tangible, correct? You see it, know it, want it, and need it. Money, or capital, is physical, and the results thereof are physical, as well; assets, homes, cars, boats, businesses, and etc. Even the online digital amount of your checking account balance is physical, and it is represented by the currency that accounts for it.

The physical appearance of money can project reputation. Someone who arrives at an event in a luxury sedan while dressed in fine apparel will get a second look; someone who steps from the city bus wearing blue jeans might not. The mere appearance of money seems to sort people who *have* and people who *have not.*

Wealth makes many friends,

But the poor is separated from his friend.

All the brothers of the poor hate him;

How much more do his friends go far from him!

He may pursue them with words, yet they abandon him.

Proverbs 19:4, 7

Yes, the results of money, capital, and wealth are physical; however, there is a spiritual side to money that can only be discerned and perceived on a deeper level—a spiritual level. As a matter of fact, I will prove to you in this chapter that, first and foremost, money is not a physical issue as much as money is a spiritual issue.

When we cross paths with people who have money (and much of it), we automatically assume a great feat has been accomplished in the lives of these people. We look at them, and we automatically think hard work, a high-ranking education, or rare talent. Whether we realize it or not, assumptions often govern a large part of our thinking; however, in many instances, assumptions can be wildly incorrect. Case in point, someone might own a spaciously beautiful home, drive a luxurious automobile, wear the latest designer apparel, and, little do we know, they inherited all they own from someone else without lifting a finger. Even better, we see someone with all the previous physical characteristics of money, yet everything they own has been charged; everything is on credit and, in truth, they own nothing. Furthermore, some people win large sums of money gambling, and what takes others a lifetime to acquire they acquire in a swift moment of anxiety and elation. Knowing how people obtain money can change our opinion of them and their money.

Here is the point: regardless of how people acquire money, a spiritual decision is first made before money comes to their possession. A spiritual decision is made to place items on credit with zero cash to back the purchases. A spiritual decision is made to place hopes and dreams on the dubious spin of a roulette wheel. Even people who serendipitously inherit money reap from the spiritual decisions sown by their predecessors.

It is safe to state that there is more to the acquisition of money than meets the eye. Furthermore, here is a truth we have all learned: not all money is obtained honestly—that is, with integrity and uprightness.

Righteous are You, O Lord, when I plead with You;

Yet let me talk with You about Your judgments.

Why does the way of the wicked prosper?

Why are those happy who deal so treacherously?

Jeremiah 12:1

We are not naive. We are aware. We see people prosper all the time in dishonest or harmful fashion, and it often seems that *nice guys finish last*. However, there are many instances of those who have labored diligently through the years, for decades, and their hard work has paid off, as well. Either way, in either instance, money is the result, but spiritual decisions were first made. The difference manifests in the security and longevity of the wealth acquired. Simply put: get-rich-quick money leaves quickly, whereas diligent money has a residual effect.

Let us approach this topic from another angle. Let us perform a backward trace to arrive at the answer we are seeking. Money (cash, currency, capital) is physical. We see it, use it, and our lives are often governed by it (even if it is in the form of your debit/credit card). The physical presence of money can derive from a physical form of collateral, meaning someone might be wealthy because they own a business that produces greatly desired goods and services, or someone might own land (property) that is abundantly plentiful and prosperous to the needs of others. Property, goods, or services generate the money a person possesses. Property is physical; you see it and walk on it. Goods and services are physical; you hold them in your hands and experience them. Furthermore, the property, goods, and services are harvested and developed by people; people such as owners, managers, employees, laborers, and etc. I think we would all agree that people are physical human beings. Therefore, all the way down the line, the wealth of an individual is made possible by something physical, such as cash, currency, capital, property, goods, services, and even people, and all of these physical manifestations come from somewhere. Furthermore, none of these physical manifestations created themselves. None of these physical manifestations are the Creator; rather, these physical manifestations have been created.

I do not mean to give you a headache by tracing this topic in such itemized fashion, but hopefully you see where I am going with this. God created the heavens and the earth, the resources of the earth, the wealth of the earth, and even those inhabiting the earth.

The earth is the Lord's, and the fullness thereof; the world, and they that dwell therein.

Psalm 24:1 KJV

,

Since we are referencing the physical and its dependency on the spiritual, the question must be asked: if everything physical has been created by God, who or what is God?

God is a Spirit: and they that worship him must worship him in spirit and in truth.

John 4:24 KJV

When I think of God as a spirit, I think of Him as the intangible and invisible Creator from whom all tangible and visible blessings flow.

Now to the King eternal, immortal, invisible, to God who alone is wise, be honor and glory forever and ever. Amen.

1 Timothy 1:17

God is the source of all things, whether physical or spiritual, whether visible or invisible, even though God is an invisible spirit. Remember, you can look for God without seeing Him, but the evidence of this same unseen God is all around you. Therefore, it is true: all things physical originate from a spiritual source. This list of the physical would include the universe, our planet, the resources of our planet, and, of course, the human race.

My point is not to overstate the obvious. Instead, I want to cause us to reflect on the original order of all things. God is the creator of all, and nothing has been created apart from Him. God is spirit; therefore, an essential, foundational, original spiritual component exists for all physical things.

Let us bring this spiritual subject to a personal level. When dealing with money, our spiritual motives have far-reaching ramifications beyond money simply leaving our hands. The love of God or the absence of the love of God within an individual will impact how they spend money. The love of God looks for ways to help those in need. The love of flesh looks for ways to satisfy oneself. Spiritual decisions are made, and physical results are yielded.

The acquisition and use of money are spiritual issues before they are physical issues, and the manifestation of right or wrong motives will inevitably rise to the surface.

It is an unrighteous spiritual decision to steal.

"You shall not steal."

Exodus 20:15

It is a righteous spiritual decision to get a job.

If anyone will not work, neither shall he eat.

2 Thessalonians 3:10

It is an unrighteous spiritual decision to be lazy. It is a righteous spiritual decision to labor diligently.

The soul of a lazy man desires, and has nothing;

But the soul of the diligent shall be made rich.

Proverbs 13:4

It is an unrighteous spiritual decision to selfishly hoard.

Do not love the world or the things in the world. If anyone loves the world, the love of the Father is not in him.

1 John 2:15

It is a righteous spiritual decision to give.

The wicked borrows and does not repay.

But the righteous shows mercy and gives.

Psalm 37:21

Obviously, there are those who are physically unable to work. The preceding scriptures speak to those who can but will not work, and there is a difference between the two examples. The point of this chapter is this: long before property is purchased, homes are built, cars are detailed, educations are obtained, and careers are chosen, spiritual decisions are made. Once spiritual decisions are made, physical results are produced, which breed other physical results, which breed other physical results. Money is neutral. How money is used is inevitable. It all begins with issues of the heart. Spiritual decisions, whether righteous or unrighteous, assign money.

The truth is, whether you accept the truth or not, you will earn, manage, and invest money while submitting to one of two ways: God's way or your way. The ways of God are concrete, fixed, immutable, and everlasting; God being the One who has created all things, including the wealth of the world. Your ways might work temporarily, but the end result is not guaranteed. You cannot possibly predict what will happen next in the world in which we live, and what happens in this world will affect your money—whether you want it to or not.

Furthermore, the negative motives with which we earn, manage, and invest money can be as detrimental to us as a lack of money can be. Please, always remember: what we sow, we reap; I promise. In fact, it does not matter if I promise it. God promises it.

Do not be deceived, God is not mocked; for whatever a man sows, that he will also reap.

Galatians 6:7

My goal is not to instill fear. My goal is to let you know that the way in which we earn, manage, and invest money is a serious matter, and our money will go where our spiritual decisions dictate. Therefore, the best spiritual decision for all of us is to connect with the invisible God from whom all physical blessings stream. I understand this might be a disappointing concept to some of you who have difficulty connecting to an invisible God. This is where the word *faith* comes back into play. You must have faith that God is who He states He is, and that He is, by far, the best option for your life, including the best option for your money.

Remember:

But without faith it is impossible to please Him, for he who comes to God must believe that He is, and that He is a rewarder of those who diligently seek Him.

Hebrews 11:6

There is no sidestepping faith in God. If you want to progress past this point, you must be willing to trust the ways of God and accept Him as He is at this moment. He will accept you as you are at this moment. The question is will you accept Him?

Exercising faith in God does not mean you have all the answers. Instead, faith in God means you trust He has the answers, and He will reveal the answers to you as you grow in Him. God will never physically reveal Himself to you; although, He will show you evidence of Him. Moreover, even when God reveals His evidence to you, it will still be your decision whether or not to receive the evidence of God by faith. As a matter of fact, Jesus was the physical evidence of God sent to earth for all mankind. Have you accepted Jesus?

The opportunity is yours to choose God by faith. Once you make the spiritual decision to accept God and the ways of God by faith, this spiritual decision will begin to yield physical results in your life, even regarding your money. As are all issues in life, money is first a spiritual issue before it is a physical issue.

Chapter Four

God Desires….

God desires the best for us. Good news such as this is worth repeating: God desires the best for us. He loves us.

I desire the best for my children. Furthermore, the love I feel for my children (my human, imperfect love) is but a shadow, a byproduct of the love God has for me; His love is perfect. How much more evidence is necessary for the love of God to be proven: the creation of our lives, the resources on earth necessary to live and breathe, our family and friends to enjoy in fullness? Again, how much more evidence is necessary for the love of God to be proven? What more could He had given than Jesus, His only Son?

Jesus is the ultimate gift of God. Nothing of greater value could have been given. There is nothing else to be stated on the matter. When God gave Jesus, He gave everything. Yes, when God gave Jesus, God gave everything because when God gave Jesus, God gave God; God gave Himself.

In the beginning was the Word, and the Word was with God, and the Word was God. He was in the beginning with God. All things were made through Him, and without Him nothing was made that was made.

John 1:1-3

And to make all see what is the fellowship of the mystery, which from the beginning of the ages has been hidden in God who created all things through Jesus Christ.

Ephesians 3:9

He is the image of the invisible God, the firstborn over all creation. For by Him all things were created that are in heaven and that are on earth, visible and invisible, whether thrones or dominions or principalities or powers. All things were created through Him and for Him. And He is before all things, and in Him all things consist.

Colossians 1:15-17

God, who at various times and in various ways spoke in time past to the fathers by the prophets, has in these last days spoken to us by His Son, whom He has appointed heir of all things, through whom also He made the worlds.

Hebrews 1:1, 2

Knowing this truth, that when God gave Jesus, God gave God, is it not legitimate to state that God desires the best for us? Furthermore, if God gave Jesus, is it not legitimate to state that God desires the best for us in every area of life? Why would God suddenly and sporadically contradict His eternal nature, His nature from the beginning, and withhold blessings from us in a particular area of life?

The answer: God would not contradict His nature. This is good news to us: our God is not a suddenly changing, shifting, vacillating God. His nature is consistent. God is the same. He has always been the same. He will always be the same.

But the mercy of the Lord is from everlasting to everlasting

On those who fear Him,

And His righteousness to children's children.

Psalm 103:17

"God is not a man, that He should lie,

Nor a son of man, that He should repent.

Has He said, and will He not do?

Or has He spoken, and will He not make it good?"

Numbers 23:19

Therefore, knowing that God gave Jesus, meaning that God gave everything, meaning that God gave God, it is a mistake for us to only apply the goodness of God to certain areas of life and not every area of life. It is incorrect for us to change the nature of God without His permission. Actually, it is impossible to change the nature of God. Thus, we must not misrepresent the nature of God to others. Yes, God is a God of boundaries, restrictions, and judgment, but before these attributes God is a God of freedom, liberty, and love. Plus, He is a God to be chosen. God grants us freewill that we may choose His love, allowing us to experience liberty and freedom far beyond what this world can offer. When we refuse to choose God and obey Him with our freewill, thus willingly declining His freedom, liberty, and love, it is then that God becomes a God of judgment, because God is just and there is no side-stepping this fact.

Based on His ultimate expression of love by giving us Jesus, it is legitimate to state that God desires the best for us? Furthermore, since the nature of God is consistent, we conclude that He desires the best for us in every area of our lives.

Beloved, I pray that you may prosper in all things and be in health, just as your soul prospers.

3 John, verse 2

God desires for me to experience salvation from sin, which takes place on a spiritual level. As a matter of fact, the lifting of sin is such a wonderful experience that other forms of spiritual prosperity cannot keep from transpiring. Bitterness is plucked and joy is planted, anxiety is plucked and peace is planted, greed is plucked and contentment is planted, and etc. The good news does not end there. Eventually, the spiritual prosperity of salvation is so overwhelming that this prosperity cannot remain simply on a spiritual level. Ultimately, these forms of spiritual prosperity translate to physical forms of prosperity. When joy is found, my countenance cannot help but change. When peace is found, signs of outward stress begin to melt. When contentment is found, visible restlessness begins to dissipate. Therefore, beginning with salvation, the door opens; a door not only leading to spiritual prosperity, but spiritual prosperity translating to physical prosperity. Demeanor improves when people come to Jesus. Health improves when people come to Jesus. Relationships improve when people come to Jesus.

Remember:

Jesus said to him, "I am the way, the truth, and the life. No one comes to the Father except through Me."

John 14:6

Salvation takes place; the beginning of a journey. Life takes on new form. Life finds life. We gladly give the struggles of life to a savior who is able to handle the load.

"Come to Me, all you who labor and are heavy laden, and I will give you rest. Take My yolk upon you and learn from Me, for I am gentle and lowly in heart, and you will find rest for your souls. For My yoke is easy and My burden is light."

Matthew 11:28-30

The areas of life that were formerly confusing and muddled begin to sharpen with focus. We begin to understand the operation of the kingdom of God in this world.

"Your kingdom come.

Your will be done

On earth as it is in heaven."

Matthew 6:10

We learn these invaluable lessons from the One who created all things; the One who created the world in which we live and who created us. There is no one who could teach us any more or any better.

He (Jesus) answered and said to them, "Because it has been given to you to know the mysteries of the kingdom of heaven, but to them it has not been given."

Matthew 13:11

We come to know Jesus. We enter a personal relationship with Him. We do not enter a one-time experience with Him. Instead, we begin a journey of supernatural love and learning for the rest of our lives. The gift of salvation produces spiritual prosperity; this spiritual prosperity translates to physical prosperity. We not only embrace how to conduct our own lives, but we learn how to interact with others, as well. We learn how to conduct ourselves and love others based on the principles of the kingdom of God to which we now belong.

"By this all will know that you are My disciples, if you have love for one another."

John 13:35

It begins with salvation: belief in your heart and confession with your mouth in Jesus as your savior. Every other area of success and prosperity branches from there. The ripple effect is endless. Knowing Jesus and His ways are of such profit that the profit is endless and cannot be contained; love, joy, peace, patience, gentleness, goodness, faith, meekness, and self-control are examples. Why would God stop His benefits there?

Not only do we enter a relationship with Jesus and begin the learning process of relationships with others, but we learn to properly function in every area of life based on the principles of the kingdom of God to which we now belong. When you come to understand that all earthly resources have been created by God, and that God is now your Heavenly Father, and you are His child, you realize that you have the inside track on how to obtain and manage the resources God has placed on earth. Again, there is no one who could teach us any more or any better. His resources have been placed on earth for you to glorify God, bless others, and enjoy for yourself.

Then God said, "Let Us make man in Our image, according to Our likeness; let them have dominion over the fish of the sea, over the birds of the air, and over the cattle, over all the earth and over every creeping thing that creeps on the earth." So God created man in His own image; in the image of God He created him; male and female He created them. Then God blessed them, and God said to them, "Be fruitful and multiply; fill the earth and subdue it; have dominion over the fish of the sea, over the birds of the air, and over every living thing that moves on the earth.

Genesis 1:26-28

What does God desire? God desires for you to succeed, prosper, win, triumph, benefit, flourish, and thrive in every area of life. This has been His desire from the beginning. Why would He change now? What an opportunity you have to begin this journey and allow your life to take on new form. The void you feel in your heart exists to be filled. God desires to fill it now. When a void exists in our hearts, God sends Jesus. God sends Jesus because He sent Jesus roughly 2,000 years ago to pay the price for sin and separation from God once and for all.

Jesus shed His blood and paid a price only He could pay. Sin carried the severest of penalties: death to mankind. Not just physical death, but spiritual death—separation from God for eternity. Only one man could serve as the worthy sacrifice. Only the blood of one man could prove sufficient...and not just any man. Jesus came to earth in human form, conceived by the Holy Ghost within a virgin; therefore, the lineage from which He came was not polluted by the seed of sinful man. Jesus lived a sin-free life to die for those full of sin. Jesus gave His life on a cross; innocence punished for the guilty. Only His blood was worthy, and His blood was shed, and He became the only acceptable sacrifice, taking the place of whoever would call on the name of the Lord to be saved.

That if you confess with your mouth the Lord Jesus and believe in your heart that God has raised Him from the dead, you will be saved. For with the heart one believes unto righteousness, and with the mouth confession is made unto salvation.

Romans 10:9, 10

God desires to save you. God desires to set you free. God desires to know you. God desires for you to grow in Him. God desires to see you prosper and succeed in every area of your life. This is what God desires.

Chapter Five

An Alignment Adjustment

Beloved, I pray that you may prosper in all things and be in health, just as your soul prospers.

3 John, verse 2

The information in this book derives from the Bible, the Word of God. The Word of God is to be taken literally before the Word of God is to be taken figuratively. Mankind, through the years and in too many instances, has hurdled the literal meaning of scripture simply to arrive at a figuratively deeper, more theologically-crafted meaning to scripture.

There are two paramount points to grasp as we proceed. First, all scripture is truth.

All scripture is given by inspiration of God, and is profitable for doctrine, for reproof, for correction, for instruction in righteousness.

2 Timothy 3:16

Second, once realizing all scripture is truth, we are obligated to present scripture in truth without altering the meaning of scripture. We are to present scripture in context and totality, never adjusting or contouring scripture to meet individual motive or preference.

Be diligent to present yourself approved to God, a worker who does not need to be ashamed, rightly dividing the word of truth.

2 Timothy 2:15

These two paramount factors, all scripture is truth and all scripture must be presented in truth, are essential for the journey on which we are embarking. We must walk in the balance of biblical scripture. Let us not be guilty of omitting certain scripture for the sake of manipulation, motive, or convenience. Such practice will cause us to lose balance. Also, let us not lean too heavily on one scripture or doctrinal issue, neglecting other areas of biblical instruction. This too will cause us to live in unbalanced fashion.

How people view the relation between God and money is often unbalanced in my opinion. There are those who believe the issue should not be discussed. People might try to push the following misquotation, that "Money is the root of all evil." Again, this is incorrect. The Bible does not state that money is the root of all evil. Rather, the Bible states that the *love of money* is the root of all evil, and there is a huge difference between the two.

For the love of money is the root of all evil: which while some coveted after, they have erred from the faith, and pierced themselves through with many sorrows.

1 Timothy 6:10 KJV

Some believe the mere appearance of money leads to greed, idolatry, and materialism. Some believe Jesus was a poor man who lived a depressed and rejected life on all fronts (I will address the life of Jesus pertaining to money later in this book). Therefore, since some perceive and portray Jesus in this way, they believe followers of Jesus are to be perceived and portrayed in this way and should live in similar fashion. Again, it is important for you to please read the chapter later in this book *Was Jesus Poor?*

The other school of thought is held by those who try to distance themselves as far as possible from the previous school of thought. There has been a segment of the church, again in my opinion, that has leaned too heavily on the message of financial prosperity. I believe an inaccurate association has been linked between walking in close relationship with God and walking with large sums of money, as if you cannot have one without the other. Granted, in their defense, maybe the reason why this segment has pursued financial prosperity so zealously is because they finally realized they had been denied correct doctrinal teaching for years—most notably from the former school of thought. Therefore, they took the concept of financial prosperity and ran with it, and they just kept running.

All this brings us to this book and this chapter. We must, as children of God, walk in the balance of scripture if we are to be prosperous in every area of life. Therefore, if we have been guilty of leaning too heavily to one side regarding any scriptural issue, not just money, we need to humble ourselves and make certain we are led by the Holy Spirit of God and not the influence of mankind. This principle includes not being led of ourselves while forming our own, private interpretation of scriptural doctrine for personal gain.

Knowing this first, that no prophecy of Scripture is of any private interpretation, for prophecy never came by the will of man, but holy men of God spoke as they were moved by the Holy Spirit.

2 Peter 1:20, 21

There is no shame in admitting the following: sometimes we need an alignment adjustment. We have a golden opportunity at this moment to re-center our focus squarely on the Word of God. Let us examine the Bible for what it is: salvation given by God, and salvation includes instruction. Let us first believe the written Word of God before we believe commentary on the written Word of God. I am thankful for quality biblical commentary. I use commentaries, study Bibles, online resources, and etc. However, these biblical resources do not replace the source. The Bible is the unequivocal Word of God, and the Bible is our source for living. Let us not add anything to the Word of God, and let us not remove anything from the Word of God.

For I testify to everyone who hears the words of the prophecy of this book: If anyone adds to these things, God will add to him the plagues that are written in this book; and if anyone takes away from the words of the book of this prophecy, God shall take away his part from the Book of Life, from the holy city, and from the things which are written in this book.

Revelation 22:18, 19

As stated in the Word of God, without adding to or removing from the Word of God, what is God's desire for us as explained by the author who was inspired by the Holy Spirit?

Beloved, I pray that you may prosper in all things and be in health, just as your soul prospers.

3 John, verse 2

Yes, prosper in all things, including the area of money.

Imagine this. When God and Jesus, before the foundation of the world, discussed the plan of creation, redemption, and all the sacrifice that would be involved, I do not think the conversation went as follows:

"You know, Father," Jesus said, "I understand. I understand I have to give My life to reconcile mankind back to You and Us. I understand, because once You give mankind a choice, mankind will undoubtedly sin and fall from grace. However, Father, when I give My life to redeem Our people, I want to redeem them from...almost everything. I want to purchase their salvation with My blood. I want to purchase their healing with the stripes on My back. I want to purchase their joy, their peace of mind, their contentment, and their relationships. I want to bring them life and life more abundantly in all areas...with one exception: their money. Father, I do not want Our people to be financially prosperous. I want Our people to live in poverty all the days of their lives. I want them to struggle to make breakeven. I want them to be the tail and not the head, the borrower and not the lender, beneath and not above."

This fictitious conversation is not consistent with the nature of God, is it? Why would Jesus come to set us free in every area of life except one area? We, as the church, would be in an uproar if anyone preached that Jesus came to give freedom in every area except for our healing, except for our joy, except for our peace, or except for our relationships. Why then do we take the area of our money, which is a huge part of our lives, and remove it from the gospel equation? Why do we take the area of money and set it off to the side?

Are you in need of an alignment adjustment today? Depending on past experiences and teachings you have received, you might be leaning too heavily on one area of biblical doctrine while neglecting another. I do not know what you have been taught. However, I believe you desire the truth. Today is the day to bring your relationship with God into alignment. Today is the beginning of an alignment adjustment.

Does God desire for us to prosper? Yes. Furthermore, in what areas of life does God desire for us to prosper? Prosper in all areas and in all things. How do we know? The Word of God teaches us this truth with great transparency.

Beloved, I pray that you may prosper in all things and be in health, just as your soul prospers.

3 John, verse 2

Chapter Six

A Lesson in Contentment: Jesus Is the Cake

As well as my personal account (by the grace of God) of how I ascended to freedom from financial debt, this book contains intermittent chapters on the subject of contentment. Rather than write one, comprehensive chapter on contentment, I have chosen to pepper this book with smaller chapters to periodically serve the following reminder: contentment must be your companion as you travel through life. Contentment is an encouraging, refreshing, yet stabilizing force that holds you firmly in place as situations and people come and go. Trust me, if there is one truth I have learned in life: situations and people come and go.

Not that I speak in regard to need, for I have learned in whatever state I am, to be content.

Philippians 4:11 NKJV

Not that I speak in respect of want: for I have learned, in whatsoever state I am, therewith to be content.

Philippians 4:11 KJV

Apart from contentment, every good gift is never enough. Along with contentment, every good gift is even better.

All things are full of labor;

Man cannot express it.

The eye is not satisfied with seeing,

Nor the ear filled with hearing.

Ecclesiastes 1:8

We are often drawn to the icing of a cake. The icing is where color manifests, decorations bloom, and artistry dazzles. The icing is so enjoyable that even a swipe of the finger seems heavenly. If you are like me and your mom let you have the beaters covered in chocolate icing before the cake was ready, you can put your hand down now.

We love the icing. We even love to use the expression *the icing on the cake*. Apart from the cake, however, the icing loses its effect. Apart from the cake, the point of the icing is diminished. Apart from the cake, the icing loses its luster. Furthermore, the icing is, in the absence of the cake, simply…a pile of goo; goo which lacks definition. Sure, eating a pile of sugary goo might be enjoyable momentarily, but soon your stomach and head will begin asking questions, such as, "What are you trying to do to us?"

I know this topic is very simple, but simple can be beneficial. Apart from the cake, the icing loses its purpose.

Take our lives for example: sometimes even the greatest blessings of life can sour.

The sunshine is beautiful unless you live with depression, and it is possible to become even more depressed when the sunshine fails to encourage you despite all its glory.

Marriage is beautiful unless you have fallen out of love with one another, and it is possible to wish you had never known love in the first place.

Wealth is beautiful unless you have wasted wealth foolishly, and it is possible to wish you never had so much money in the beginning.

Jesus has been given to us by God that we may have relationship with God. Jesus serves as the living Word of God, showing us that we can connect with the Creator of the universe through Him. Jesus is the substance that holds our relationship with God together. Jesus, in other words, is the cake. He is the substance. He is the quality. He is the definition. He is the focus. He is the purpose.

The sun shines brighter when Jesus is in your heart. As a matter of fact, even when the sun does not shine there is still joy; a joy that is difficult to explain and express. Furthermore, literally and figuratively, life is good on a cloudy day when Jesus is in your heart, and on a day when the sun is shining, the sunshine becomes the icing on the cake.

You have not seen Christ, but still you love him. You cannot see him now, but you believe in him. So you are filled with a joy that cannot be explained, a joy full of glory.

1 Peter 1:8 New Century Version

Marriages are better when both the husband and wife love Jesus. Suddenly, the differences between the two are not viewed as obstacles, yet perspectives. The differences between men and women are seen for the truth, that God created man and woman differently, that the two balance one another, and where one has a weakness the other is strong. Finally, when a married couple realizes that, no matter how much they love each other, their love for God must always come first, and through their relationships with God their marriage is enhanced, guess what? Marriage becomes the icing on the cake.

Wives, submit to your own husbands, as to the Lord. Husbands, love your wives, just as Christ also loved the Church and gave Himself for her. "For this reason a man shall leave his father and mother and be joined to his wife, and the two shall become one flesh."

Ephesians 5:22, 25, 31

Wealth is much, much, much better when you understand the purpose for wealth, that we are blessed to be a blessing, that it is more blessed to give than receive, and that we are not called to hoard but to give. Also, wealth is much better when it is obtained through righteousness. Looking over your shoulder for the rest of your life is no way to live. Knowing that you had to wrong someone to prosper is no way to live.

However, when you realize you have nothing going for you in life until someone tells you that Jesus loves you, that He died for your sins, that He knows you by name, and that no amount of money can buy your salvation, and you ask Jesus to reside in your heart, it is then that the wealth of this world becomes the icing on the cake.

He who trusts in his riches will fall,

But the righteous will flourish like foliage.

Proverbs 11:28

As you know, I subtitled this book, *Depression-and-recession-proof living*. I did so since this book not only applies to money, but this book applies to every area of my life. Furthermore, the biblical precepts of this book will not only be successful when the U.S. economy suffers financial depression or recession, but these infallible precepts will be successful when my heart and mind face emotional, mental, or spiritual depression, as well. As sure as the sun rises in the east, all of us—even the happiest of us—will be confronted by depression in our lifetime. However, the peace of God which surpasses all of your human understanding will defeat depression in all its forms by the power of your faith in God, and this same power of God will keep and guard your heart and mind by Jesus Christ.

And the peace of God, which surpasses all understanding, will guard your hearts and minds through Christ Jesus.

Philippians 4:7

Apart from the cake, the icing is nothing. The icing is goo. The icing is fluff. The icing is enjoyable for a while, but the after-effects fall far short of satisfaction. Remember as you go through life: Jesus is the cake, and He causes the other blessings of life to be the icing on the cake.

Chapter Seven

Blessed to Be a Blessing

The Bible declares that God desires for us to prosper in all things, which includes the area of money. Therefore, it is essential to grasp the two-fold reason why He desires for us to prosper: to glorify God and to bless others.

Jesus said to him, "'You shall love the Lord your God with all your heart, with all your soul, and with all your mind.' This is the first and great commandment. And the second is like it: 'You shall love your neighbor as yourself.'"

Matthew 22:37-39

As I stated earlier, the nature of God is consistent. Furthermore, the nature of God is to love us. Since we are made in the image of God, and His presence resides within us, it is the desire of God for us to love one another. As a matter of fact, it is impossible for us to house the likeness and love of God and not love one another, for God is love. Our love for one another should be automatic. If the love of God resides within us, it is inevitable: we will love one another.

"A new commandment I give to you, that you love one another; as I have loved you, that you also love one another. By this all will know that you are My disciples, if you have love for one another."

John 13:34, 35

Beloved, let us love one another, for love is of God; and everyone who loves is born of God and knows God. He who does not love does not know God, for God is love.

1 John 4:7, 8

If the nature of God, therefore, does not change, and if His nature is applicable to every area of our lives, the nature of God is applicable to the way we view money, as well. What is the first great command cited by Jesus? Love God. What is the second great command cited by Jesus? Love others. If the love of God resides within us, we will inevitably love one another. Furthermore, if the nature of God is consistent and applicable to every area of our lives, including how we earn, manage, and invest money, His will for our money is to glorify Him and bless others.

Our health is meant to glorify God, our relationships are meant to glorify God, and, yes, the way we earn, manage, and invest money is meant to glorify God, as well. Not only glorify God, but glorify God and bless others. We should uphold the two commandments cited by

Jesus, love God and love others, in all that we do, including the way we earn, manage, and invest money.

When I am in good health, I am a living testimony that God is good, and my good health encourages others that what God does for one He will do for another: God is glorified and others are blessed.

Then Peter opened his mouth, and said, Of a truth I perceive that God is no respecter of persons.

Acts 10:34 KJV

When my marriage is in good standing, I am a living testimony that God is good, and my marriage encourages others that what God does for one He will do for another: God is glorified and others are blessed.

Then Peter opened his mouth, and said, Of a truth I perceive that God is no respecter of persons.

Acts 10:34 KJV

When my financial position is in good standing, I am a living testimony that God is good, and my good financial position encourages others that what God does for one He will do for another: God is glorified and others are blessed.

Then Peter opened his mouth, and said, Of a truth I perceive that God is no respecter of persons.

Acts 10:34 KJV

Furthermore, when my health, relationships, and financial position are doing well, I am not only able to tell people that these areas are well, but I am able to give to others out of these areas. I am able to help carry their groceries when I am in good health. My wife and I are able to sit down with them over dinner and share the experiences God has given us when our marriage is well. I am able to financially give to people who are in need when my financial position is well. I am blessed to be a blessing. Every blessing in my life is held to the same standard and shares the same criteria: all blessings from God will glorify God and bless others. I must love God and love others, even with my money.

I will make you a great nation;

I will bless you

And make your name great;

And you shall be a blessing.

Genesis 12:2

Obviously, when you study this text in Genesis, the Lord was speaking to Abram who later became Abraham; the Father of the Nation of Israel. Furthermore, when I reference this scripture, I am not taking it out of context to meet my desire, nor am I using this scripture to punch a meal ticket in the name of prosperity.

Please allow me to explain. God saw fit for Abraham to be the father of the Nation of Israel. Jesus is of the lineage of David who is of the lineage of Abraham.

The book of the genealogy of Jesus Christ, the Son of David, the Son of Abraham.

Matthew 1:1

Jesus (an eventual descendant of Abraham), through the salvation He has provided, has opened the kingdom of God and the blessings of the kingdom of God to both the Jewish people and non-Jewish people, otherwise known as Gentiles.

That the blessing of Abraham might come upon the Gentiles in Christ Jesus, that we might receive the promise of the Spirit through faith.

Galatians 3:14

The blessing of Abraham from whom Jesus derived is an all-inclusive blessing. God desires for us to be blessed and walk in His blessing in every area of life.

Beloved, I pray that you may prosper in all things and be in health, just as your soul prospers.

3 John, verse 2

Therefore, by the mercy of God, all people who come to God through faith in Jesus are found acceptable in the eyes of God and, by the mercy of God, are eligible to receive the blessings of God that were offered to Abraham.

For what does the Scripture say? "Abraham believed God, and it was accounted to him for righteousness."

Romans 4:3

For "whoever calls on the name of the Lord shall be saved."

Romans 10:13

For I speak to you Gentiles; inasmuch as I am an apostle to the Gentiles, I magnify my ministry. And if some of the branches were broken off, and you, being a wild olive tree, were grafted in among them, and with them became a partaker of the root and fatness of the olive tree, do not boast against the branches. But if you do boast, remember that you do not support the root, but the root supports you.

Romans 11:13, 17, 18

Here is a paramount truth to grasp. The faith-believing Gentiles (non-Jewish people) have been grafted into the kingdom of God through Jesus Christ and are eligible to receive the blessing of Abraham given by God. Please note: this does allow for or give place to *replacement theology*. In other words, as a non-Jewish person who has accepted Jesus Christ, I am not suddenly qualified for the blessing of God at the expense of the Jewish people being disqualified from the blessing of God; far from it. Instead, we walk jointly in the blessing of God as Jewish and non-Jewish people alike. God loves Israel, and God is faithful to Israel to this day, and God will be faithful to Israel tomorrow. We as non-Jewish believers only partake of the blessing. We do not overtake the blessing, and there is a huge difference between the two.

Furthermore, the precept of receiving the blessing of God does not enable us to teach a false doctrine of *gravy-train prosperity*. No. We must realize that with provision comes responsibility. We must understand the purpose for the blessing of Abraham. Let us walk in the balance of the scriptures.

I will make you a great nation;

I will bless you

And make your name great;

And you shall be a blessing.

Genesis 12:2

Not only are we to be blessed, but we are to be a blessing; a blessing in all areas of life. We, as children of God, as adopted children and descendants of Abraham, are called to bring the gospel message of Jesus Christ to the world. We are to tell the world of His love. We are to physically demonstrate the love of God to the world. Since we are blessed with the blessing of Abraham to prosper, we accept that with provision comes responsibility, and we accept the responsibility to be a blessing. Many people rejoice over the blessing of Abraham, but we must also recognize the responsibility that comes with the blessing: again, we are blessed to be a blessing. Furthermore, we are blessed to be a blessing in every area of life. Someone who selfishly desires the blessing of Abraham to selfishly hoard the blessing is not qualified to receive the blessing. Our purpose in life is to glorify God and bless others, and this includes the area of our money.

Here is an important question to ponder: why do you want to prosper financially? Why do you desire financial success? What is the ultimate reason in your heart and mind to flourish financially? Do you harbor a selfishly-driven desire to prosper financially? Is it to be well known, much seen, or to gain much notoriety? Is it to be rich enough to be left alone? Remember, He or she who cannot love others does not have the love of God in his or her heart.

This is an ideal opportunity to consider our motives before proceeding. Remember: we are blessed to be a blessing. We are called to love God and love others, and this includes how we earn, manage, and invest money. Take inventory of your motives to prosper before you seek one more dollar in life. We are to glorify God, and we are blessed to be a blessing.

Chapter Eight

The Economy of God versus the Economy of the World

As I stated at the beginning of this book: I'm not a millionaire, but I'm debt free. Therefore, every aspect of this book played a role in getting me to this point in my life. Furthermore, not only can the information in this book work for you, the information in this book can work in any financial climate. The information in this book is recession-proof. Should the U.S. economy trend downward for several years, this information will still work. The information in this book is depression-proof, as well. Should the U.S. economy hit rock bottom and split the rock in half, this information will still work.

How and why will this information work and continue to work? The precepts in this book are founded on the eternal, infallible Word of God. The Word of God is not going anywhere, and the kingdom of God is not going anywhere, and if I were you, given the unpredictable economic landscape of the U.S. and the world, I would apply these recession-and-depression-proof precepts ASAP. Do you need further proof that these precepts work? I am your proof; just a regular guy...with regular grades in school...from a regular city in the Midwest, raised in a regular family of hardworking people.

It is paramount to understand that money is a spiritual issue before it is a physical issue. As I explained earlier, the physical wealth we see (capital, property, goods and services) were created by a God we cannot see. We constantly see the evidence of God, but we do not see God. This is faith: believing based on the evidence of that which is unseen.

Now faith is the substance of things hoped for, the evidence of things not seen.

Hebrews 11:1

I know people struggle with the concept of faith; although, I believe many people have more faith than they realize. Simply put: if you recognize wind on a windy day, you have the basics of faith. Think on this for a few moments. You do not see wind. Instead, you see the evidence of wind thanks to waving branches or rustling leaves, but you cannot see wind. However, you have enough faith to believe in wind you cannot see based on evidence you can see. Again, I use the example of wind because if you understand the properties of wind, you are well on your way to understanding the properties of faith.

Here are the words of Jesus:

"Do not marvel that I said to you, 'You must be born again.' The wind blows where it wishes, and you hear the sound of it, but cannot tell where it comes from and where it goes. So is everyone who is born of the Spirit."

John 3:7, 8

I know people desire empirical, unequivocal evidence before they believe in someone or something. If you are the type of person who gathers one-hundred percent of the evidence before making every decision in life, I congratulate you. You must be a very accurate and exacting individual who gives diligent attention to every detail in life. I will also surmise that—at the rate you are going—you probably average one major decision for every ten years of living. Very few times in life do we see all the facts, proof, and evidence enough to satisfy every curiosity and calm every fear before making an important decision. Instead, many decisions in life are made by faith.

It is by faith that we lunge into the unknown. It is by faith that we endeavor toward new inventions. It is by faith that we challenge and compel ourselves to do greater, learn more, and understand beyond ourselves. Finally, it is by faith, and only by faith, that we make ourselves vulnerable to the infinite wisdom of God and grow in continual relationship with Him for all of our days.

Faith must be present from beginning to end in our relationships with God. Faith is not applied on a one-time basis, such as when we exercise faith to receive salvation. The moment of salvation is not the end of the journey; it is the beginning. Furthermore, faith must be applied in our relationships with God at all times and in all areas. Therefore, if our lives belong to God, including every area of our lives, why then would we operate the financial area of our lives by any other concept than faith? Why would our faith in God exclude the area of money (the earning, managing, and investing thereof)? We have faith in the Word of God, which means we have faith in the ways of God. Therefore, our faith pertains to the area of our money, as well.

Let us, with all of this stated, transfer the precepts and principles of faith in God and faith in the Word of God to right here, right now. We hear the word *economy* used constantly. The word *economy* often refers to the financial state of the world or a particular nation. I live in the United States of America. Therefore, I cannot walk down the street without hearing information or someone's opinion regarding the U.S. economy on a daily basis.

As a matter of fact, the world or national economy encompasses much more than just money. The economies of nations are affected by a number of variables, including the value of currencies, the health of large corporations and small businesses, unemployment rates, inflation, cost of living, interest rates, predictions on where the economy is going, data on where the economy has been, tourism, terrorism, natural disasters, and the list is endless. Depending on the impact of these variables, not to mention how these variables work in concert together or against each other, it is legitimate to state that the economy of a nation can be fragile. The economy of a nation can thrive and flourish for years, so much so that an economy can absorb a negative impact and keep going. However, the economy of a nation can sputter and wallow for years, so much so that it requires several positive factors and years to get an economy back on track. Therefore, it is legitimate to state that since so many variables contribute to the status of an economy, and since we live in a world that is unpredictable at the very least from one day to the next, the idea of an unstable economy can easily spark fear in the hearts of the masses.

I would like to fast-forward and interject some good news at this juncture. Yes, the world has an economy, and nations have economies; however, the kingdom of God has an economy. Better yet, the economy of the kingdom of God is not struggling, neither is the economy of the kingdom of God subject to the same fearful variables as the economy of the world. Rather, the economy of the kingdom of God is safe, dependable, consistent, and the economy of the kingdom of God is not in recession because the kingdom of God is not in recession. The kingdom of God and its principles are held in place, held in tact by the authoritative Word of God, and the Word of God is overseen by God Himself.

"Heaven and earth will pass away, but My words will by no means pass away."

Matthew 24:35

Then the Lord said to me, "You have seen well, for I am ready to perform My word."

Jeremiah 1:12

The best choice we can make in an unstable, fragile, unpredictable world, which has an unstable, fragile, unpredictable economy, is get connected with the safe, dependable, consistent kingdom of God, which has a safe, dependable, consistent economy.

"Do not lay up for yourselves treasures on earth, where moth and rust destroy and where thieves break in and steal; but lay up for yourselves treasures in heaven, where neither moth nor rust destroys and where thieves do not break in and steal. For where your treasure is, there your heart will be also."

Matthew 6:19-21

If you are asking me if I believe in heaven, I will answer you without hesitation: absolutely! I believe in heaven, not only as the place of my eternal destination, but I believe in the principles of heaven, as well. Please let me explain. My Heavenly Father has all dominion in heaven. God governs heaven with sovereignty. Heaven runs according to schedule as He assures it so. The story does not end there. God has all dominion in both heaven and earth. Obviously I live on earth, and since God has granted dominion to mankind on earth along with the institution of freewill, I have the power to either submit to the principles of this world or submit to the principles of heaven. Furthermore, I have dominion, ability, and power to enlist the principles of heaven on earth.

"In this manner, therefore, pray:

Our Father in heaven,

Hallowed be Your name.

Your kingdom come.

Your will be done

On earth as it is in heaven."

Matthew 6:9, 10

Obviously, Matthew 6:9-10 are very familiar words spoken by Jesus. Hopefully, when you speak this prayer you do not speak it mindlessly from a heart of religion. Hopefully, you have dissected this prayer and come in agreement with the intent. "God, Your will be done on earth as it is in heaven." Heaven is not a place of sin, sickness, evil, dejection, or rejection. No. Heaven is a place of complete restoration between God and mankind; the place where God and mankind live in loving relationship with one another. Also, heaven is not a place of lack, poverty, or recession. Construction of the streets of gold was not purchased on credit. The adorning precious stones of heaven are not imitations. I will write the words again: heaven is not a place of sin, sickness, evil, dejection, rejection, lack, poverty, or recession.

Therefore, when we apply faith in the principles of the economy of God instead of the economy of this world, and because of the dominion, ability, and power God has given us as His children, we are able to implement the economy of the kingdom of God on earth as it is in heaven.

The Spirit Himself bears witness with our spirit that we are children of God, and if children, then heirs—heirs of God and joint heirs with Christ, if indeed we suffer with Him, that we may also be glorified together.

Romans 8:16, 17

Remember our alignment adjustment: not only are we heirs of God and joint heirs with Jesus pertaining to salvation, but we are entitled to every benefit under the covering of salvation, which includes every area of life, which includes our financial welfare. Why? We are called to glorify God and bless others. We are blessed to be a blessing.

As we wade farther into this topic, it is essential for us to understand that there are two economic systems at work in the world today, and the spiritual always precedes the physical. Case in point: if we go back to the beginning, we read that God had a much better lifestyle in mind for mankind in the Garden of Eden. In the Garden of Eden, fellowship with God was connected. Creation was uninfected. Food, clothing, and shelter were all in abundance. Enter sin: disobedience by the act of freewill. In fact, even before the initial act of sin was committed with a physical response, sin took root in the heart of mankind on a spiritual level. A spiritual decision preceded the physical result. What happened next? Fellowship with God became disconnected. Creation became infected. Food, clothing, and shelter were now at a premium, requiring the labor of mankind to procure these essentials in life, even in the sweat of his face.

Then to Adam He (God) said, "Because you have heeded the voice of your wife, and have eaten from the tree of which I commanded you, saying, 'You shall not eat of it':

"Cursed is the ground for your sake;

In toil you shall eat of it

All the days of your life.

Both thorns and thistles it shall bring forth for you,

And you shall eat the herb of the field.

In the sweat of your face you shall eat bread

Till you return to the ground,

For out of it you were taken;

For dust you are,

And to dust you shall return."

Genesis 3:17-19

First and foremost, let us not lose the context of the preceding scripture. Listening to his wife was not Adam's sin. Rather, surrendering to sin was Adam's sin. Even so, Adam had every opportunity to remain obedient, but he sinned of his own freewill.

The consequence of sin immediately took effect. Cursed was the ground for Adam's (mankind's) sake; cursed for him and all who followed after him, even us. Toil and hard labor were subsequently mandated in the presence of thorns and thistles. There was, in short, a new system born and at work; the system of a fallen world, which included a new economic system under its umbrella. Sin affects every area of life. Sin affects our minds, our emotions, even the health in our physical bodies. Furthermore, all who would follow after Adam would be affected by sin, including the introduction of a new economic system of this fallen world.

Once sin entered the world, we were all subject to sin.

For all have sinned and fall short of the glory of God.

Romans 3:23

This worldly economic system spanned from Old Testament to New Testament, and this worldly economic system was evident and at work when Satan confronted and tempted Jesus.

Again, the devil took Him (Jesus) up on an exceedingly high mountain, and showed Him all the kingdoms of the world and their glory (including their economic wealth). And he said to Him, "All these things I will give You if You will fall down and worship me." Then Jesus said to

him, "Away with you, Satan! For it is written, 'You shall worship the Lord your God, and Him only you shall serve.'"

Matthew 4:8-10

Satan is the ultimate opportunist, and Satan took opportunity to employ sin against mankind once mankind sinned. Those who are enslaved to sin are ultimately enslaved to Satan, whether they want to be or not, whether they know it or not—I know I was.

He who sins is of the devil, for the devil has sinned from the beginning. For this purpose the Son of God was manifested, that He might destroy the works of the devil.

1 John 3:8

There is the good news! There is the relief! There is the breakthrough! Yes, mankind sinned, and, no, this was not God's original intent for mankind. However, even though mankind sinned, the sin of mankind did not pollute the character of God one iota. Instead, once fellowship between God and mankind was severed, because God is holy and cannot tolerate sin, nor can the sinful stand in His presence, God offered an alternative to the enslavement of sin.

Jesus said to him, "I am the way, the truth, and the life. No one comes to the Father except through Me."

John 14:6

Faith in God through Jesus preserves those who repent. Furthermore, just as sin was destined to affect every area of our lives, Jesus provided freedom from sin. Thus, this freedom from sin affects every area of our lives in reverse. Our lives are no longer cursed under the bondage of sin. Our lives are blessed under the blood of Jesus. Thus, we become His children. Thus, we become part of the kingdom of God. Thus, even though we live in this fallen world, we are ultimately not of this world.

Jesus said:

"If you were of the world, the world would love its own. Yet because you are not of the world, but I chose you out of the world, therefore the world hates you."

John 15:19

"I (Jesus) do not pray that You (God) should take them out of the world, but that You should keep them from the evil one. They are not of the world, just as I am not of the world."

John 17:15, 16

And do not be conformed to this world, but be transformed by the renewing of your mind, that you may prove what is that good and acceptable and perfect will of God.

Romans 12:2

Let's put it all together. I am in this world but not of this world. As a child of God, I am in this world, but my salvation is not of this world. Furthermore, if God grants me every possible blessing and gift as a byproduct of salvation, I am in this world, but my joy is not of this world. I am in this world, but my peace of mind is not of this world. My wife and I are in this world, but the blessing of our marriage is not of this world. Therefore, I am in this world, but my money is not of this world. I am in this world, but the protection of my money is not from this world. I am in this world, but as a child of God, as part of the kingdom of God, the increase of my money is not of this world.

Remember:

Beloved, I pray that you may prosper in all things and be in health, just as your soul prospers.

3 John, verse 2

Every good gift and every perfect gift is from above, and comes down from the Father of lights (God), with whom there is no variation or shadow of turning.

James 1:17

If it helps you visualize this point, you, as a child of God, are under an impenetrable bubble, an ultra-protective layer, shielded by the supernatural strength of God. As a child of God, you are beneath an iron umbrella which deflects and redirects casualty and catastrophe.

And we know that all things work together for good to those who love God, to those who are the called according to His purpose.

Romans 8:28

Your salvation is secure as long as you willingly remain under the offered protection of God. You are part of the kingdom of God. The kingdom of God has an economy, and, as long as you operate in the principles of the economy of the kingdom of God, your money is in this world but not of this world. Do you need further proof? I am your proof; just a regular guy...with regular grades in school...from a regular city in the Midwest, raised in a regular family of hardworking people.

How did I do it? I put my faith in the God who ultimately rules heaven and earth. I invested my money in the economy of God.

The earth is the Lord's, and the fullness thereof; the world, and they that dwell therein.

Psalm 24:1 KJV

The earth does not belong to anyone else but the Lord. The earth does not belong to any national government or corporation, such as the United States of America, China, Walmart, Apple, Chevron, or Exxon. I am not degrading these countries or corporations. Rather, I am stating the fact that the earth belongs to the Lord. The Lord has not changed. The Lord is still in power. The Lord has always been in power, and the Lord will always be in power. This should be good news to you today: no matter what happens regarding world events, no matter what happens regarding rising and falling financial markets, regardless of who is elected as world leaders or the leaders of super-power nations, the Lord is still in charge, still in power, still sovereign, and He is not going anywhere.

The earth is the Lord's, and the fullness thereof; the world, and they that dwell therein.

Psalm 24:1 KJV

Chapter Nine

The Economy of God verses the Economy of The World Continued: Two Profiles

Keeping in mind that there are two economics systems at work in the world today, the economy of this world and the economy of God, let us now compare these two economies.

Here is a profile of the economy of the world:

1) The economy of the world is unstable

As I stated earlier, we often think of sheer monetary achievement and effectiveness when evaluating the economy of a nation or the world. Nevertheless, there are numerous non-wealth-related issues that dictate the success or failure of an economy: agricultural success or failure, terrorism, earthquakes, tsunamis, hurricanes, tornados, wildfires, wars, rumors of war, and etc. Once you consider these variables, it is legitimate to state that the world economy is unstable and fragile. Even the death or overthrow of certain world leaders can dictate economic rise or fall. These issues are non-monetary issues. I have yet to cite the monetary variables that can affect an economy: value of national currencies, plunging or rising home mortgage rates, plunging or rising stock market rates, cost of living, inflation, and etc.

2) The economy of the world is unpredictable

I realize that instability and unpredictability go hand in hand. Nevertheless, even if all the variables for a prosperous economy are in alignment, there are still no guarantees that the outcome will be positive. Raise taxes, cut taxes, expand benefits, restrict benefits, government stimulus or no stimulus; there are no guarantees regarding economic outcome. There is conjecture, speculation, and hope, but there are no guarantees. Even the best economic playbooks have failed to put points on the board throughout history. The unpredictable nature of the world economy is difficult to harness.

3) The economy of the world is unfair

Please do not misunderstand what I am about to write. I do not believe in socialism. I do not believe in even distribution of wealth and property. I believe in a reward system. God rewards based on individual merit, and I am of the same belief.

Bluntly put: the economy of the world benefits some people but not all people. There is a large gap between the rich and the poor. Granted, there are explanations for this truth. Still we live in a world where opulence and hunger inhabit the same planet. You might have been taught as I have been taught: work hard and earn what you want in this world. However, the economy of this world does not automatically reward hard work. There are some who have worked extremely hard and still have little. There are some who have hardly worked and yet have much. Some start their lives with nothing. Some start their lives with everything. Again, it is clear to see that the spiritual decisions of others affect us, even before we enter the world. There are both righteous and wicked leaders who sit in high places of government over the nations. Such leaders twiddle the destinies of others among their fingers. Some leaders through history have brought freedom and prosperity to those they have governed. Others have withheld the essentials of life from the masses of humanity, driving hope from the countenance of the people with a cruel rod of control.

Furthermore, the economy of this world gives you little opportunity to make a difference. Sure, you can do your best, work hard, work extra, save money, and invest money. However, at the end of the day, there are no guarantees. What happens when you want to work, but no one is hiring? What happens when you want to work extra, but your job is not offering overtime? What happens when you want to invest money, but the markets are losing value instead of gaining value? It is not enough to have a strong work ethic with good intentions. Instead, we must make certain that our strong work ethic and good intentions are channeled to a place where a return is guaranteed.

4) Here is the motto of the world economy: every man and woman for themselves; get what you can while you can.

Do what you must. Use what tactics you must. Wrong who you must for your own interest and benefit. You must protect yourself at the end of the day with no regard for anyone else when push comes to shove; get what you can while you can. All I need to use is one word to describe the economy of this world: selfish.

Contrastingly, here is the profile of the economy of God:

1) The economy of God is stable

How do we know that the economy of God is stable? God is stable. The kingdom of God has the characteristics of God Himself: eternal, never changing, the same from generation to generation. Simply put, the existence of God is not regressing nor in recession. We need never be concerned for the welfare of God. Thus, we need never be concerned for the economy of God. All we need to do is trust and apply His economic principles to our lives. If you are His child, this is encouraging and comforting news to you.

Remember,

"God is not a man, that He should lie,

Nor a son of man, that He should repent.

Has He said, and will He not do?

Or has He spoken, and will He not make it good?"

Numbers 23:19

2) The economy of God is predictable

God outlines in His Word what will happen if you choose to be part of the righteousness of His economy.

In the house of the righteous there is much treasure,

But in the revenue of the wicked is trouble.

Proverbs 15:6

The economic principles of the kingdom of God are built on the eternal Word of God. The Word of God supplies precepts that have been proven to work for generation after generation.

He has declared to His people the power of His works,

In giving them the heritage of the nations.

The works of His hands are verity and justice;

All His precepts are sure.

They stand fast forever and ever,

And are done in truth and uprightness.

Psalm 111:6-8

We will discuss the following topic later in this book, but this is a good juncture in which to introduce the following truth. Do not judge the ways and precepts of God based on immediate, physical results. Instead, judge the ways and precepts of God based on reliable results over the course of your life. Furthermore, if you consistently apply the principles of the economy of God, because of the faithfulness of God and the effectiveness of His Word, the results of the economy of God will eventually overtake the results of the economy of the world for your life, and no one will be able to stop this from taking place. I repeat: if you consistently apply the principles of the economy of God, the results of the economy of God will eventually overtake the results of the economy of the world for your life, and no one will be able to stop this from taking place.

3) The economy of God is fair

The economy of God benefits whoever will come to God and apply His ways and principles to their lives.

Moreover the profit of the land is for all; even the king is served from the field.

Ecclesiastes 5:9

This is good news for everyone. The principles of the economy of God can and will work for all; this includes you. Whether you come from a wealthy family or not, whether you live on the good side of the tracks or not, whether you have a P.H.D. or not, the principles of the economy of God can and will work for you. It is not a matter of having an extensive career resume. Instead, it is a matter of applying the principles of the Word of God. God is fair to all. God is open to all. God desires for all to come to Him, submit to him, learn from Him, and live under His blessing.

If you are willing and obedient,

You shall eat the good of the land.

Isaiah 1:19

Please read the following closely to eliminate any confusion. I am not downplaying the significance or importance of having an impressive career resume or educational degree. Many have worked very diligently to obtain such credentials in life, and they are to be commended. As a matter of fact, the diligence these people have applied has given them an inside track to obtaining wealth in this world. We reap what we sow. My point for this chapter is to highlight the two economic systems at work in the world today. Again, these systems are the economy of this world and the economy of God. Our goal should be to operate in the economy of God;

thus, these godly results will eventually overtake the results of the economy of this world for our lives, and I will give you firsthand, true-life examples of what God has done in my life during this book. It is very important to note, however, that the economy of this world is a physical system that lives and breathes, and, because we live in this world, we are impacted by the effects of this world's economy. Therefore, we must learn to offset and eventually supersede this impact by consistently implementing the principles of God by faith. Ultimately, I assure you, the effects of the economy of God will overwhelm the effects of the economy of the world in your life.

I needed to explain the previous truth to explain the following truth. The economy of this world honors accomplishments of this world. The economy of this world honors impressive career resumes, lofty educational degrees, members of wealthy families, members of elite society, and etc. It is true: there are different ways to get ahead. However, not everyone has access to these same beneficial avenues. Furthermore, people who have access to these avenues may not see the need to apply the precepts of God since they have found such success living in their own fashion.

Let it be known: God desires for children to work diligently and assemble impressive career resumes, as well. God desires for His children to be highly educated when He opens the doors for them to do so. God desires for wealthy, influential families to further the blessings of the kingdom of God to those who have not had the same opportunities. God, in short, can use what you give Him to use. Please understand: if you have two hands and a solid work ethic and that's it, God can use you, and you will see success if you apply the ways of God to your life. However, the more you give God to use, the more He can multiply what you give Him.

4) Here is the motto of the economy of God: you are blessed to be a blessing (selfless...not selfish)

The merciful man does good for his own soul,

But he who is cruel troubles his own flesh.

Proverbs 11:17

Here is the question of the hour: how do we enter the economy of God? I will explore this matter in great detail in the following chapter. However, before we can enter the economy of the kingdom of God, we must first enter the kingdom of God. How do we enter the kingdom of God? We enter the kingdom of God by faith in God through the blood of Jesus.

All the benefits to being a child of God can be yours. The kingdom of God is available to whoever will come and receive. Furthermore, this decision represents much more than mere money. This is salvation. This is eternal life. This is physical healing, spiritual healing, and emotional healing. This is peace, joy, contentment, and the list is endless. If you have never asked Jesus to be your savior, if you have never asked Him to take residence in your heart, now is the time. Join me in the making the best decision of your life.

Yes, God wants you to enter the economy of His kingdom, but first He wants you to enter His kingdom.

Chapter Ten

How to Enter the Economy of God: Bring the Tithe

For all of you hardcore, nuts-and-bolts, pragmatic, dollars-and-cents thinkers, don't worry: we will get to all that fun stuff later. Please remember in the meantime: the spiritual always precedes the physical, thus spiritual decisions yield physical results. I share this with you to help brace you: the next several chapters will underscore fundamental spiritual steps to ultimate debt freedom.

First and foremost, let us understand one another: God cares for you, and God is concerned with every area of your life.

Casting all your care upon Him, for He cares for you.

1 Peter 5:7

Let us understand this truth, as well: God cares more for you than He cares for your money. Yes, God cares for your financial position, your relationships, your physical healing, and etc. However, God cares most for you. God cares for your eternal salvation more than any one area of your life. Yes, He has great plans for you; although, these plans will never work against the greater good of your eternal salvation.

"If your right eye causes you to sin, pluck it out and cast it from you; for it is more profitable for you that one of your members perish, than for your whole body to be cast into hell."

Matthew 5:29

When you read the biblical text preceding Matthew 5:29, you will find that Jesus is referencing a man looking on a woman with lust. Thus, Jesus is stating if you have a problem lusting after women, it is better to lose an eye and make it to heaven as opposed to allowing your eye to sin and your entire body entering hell. Obviously, Jesus is figuratively speaking here. He does not desire for anyone to physically harm themselves by removing an eye. Let me state it like this: if you have a problem lusting after women on cable or satellite television, get rid of cable or satellite. It is better to enter heaven without cable television than enter hell with cable television. Thus, if you struggle with lusting after money and materialism, it is better to enter heaven in ultra-humbleness with little to your name than have great riches and enter hell.

God values most the prosperity of your soul, knowing that every area of life will branch from there.

Beloved, I pray that you may prosper in all things and be in health, just as your soul prospers.

3 John, verse 2

Once you enter the kingdom of God through faith in the blood sacrifice of Jesus, you are ready to embrace all God has for you; yes, including financial stability and success.

Here is some information we must know regarding the character of God: God makes agreements. God honors agreements. God enjoys agreements. Did you know God is welcoming you to make an agreement with Him at this moment? He desires to enter an agreement with you, not only regarding your salvation but regarding your money, as well. God would delight to enter an agreement, a bond, and a covenant with you this day. Agreements with God, in a way, are similar to agreements made between individuals to this degree: there is something expected of both parties. One person is responsible to do this and the other person is responsible to do that. The wonderful truth regarding God and His agreements: God always keeps His agreements.

For all the promises of God in Him are Yes, and in Him Amen, to the glory of God through us.

2 Corinthians 1:20

Did you know that if you honor God with your money, God will honor your money? I explained the two financial systems at work in the previous chapter: the economy of the world and the economy of God. Also, I stated that if you consistently apply the principles of the economy of God to your money (the earning, managing, and investing thereof), the effects of the economy of God will eventually overtake the effects of the economy of the world for your life, and no one will be able to stop this from taking place.

Therefore, let us answer the huge, overarching question before us. Let us determine the starting point to entering the economy of the kingdom of God.

"Bring all the tithes into the storehouse,

That there may be food in My house,

And try Me now in this,"

Says the Lord of Hosts,

"If I will not open for you the windows of heaven

And pour out for you such blessing

That there will not be room enough to receive it."

Malachi 3:10

We enter the economy of God by first bringing the tithe to Him; bringing God the tithe is the first step toward success in the economy of God. Bringing God the tithe is a step of obedience. Bringing God the tithe is a step of admission, whereby we acknowledge that everything we have comes from God, and we will give back to Him what is rightfully due Him as our provider.

The word *tithe* means a tenth part; otherwise, ten percent. When I give God ten percent of my increase, I enter an agreement with Him. I give Him what He is due, and He provides what I need to live. Ultimately, His provision is such that there will not be room enough to receive just one form of His provision. What do I mean by one form of provision? The provision of God's blessing is abundant enough that His *provision* becomes *provisions*. Thus, His provisions positively affect other areas of my life, even beyond my money, which is wonderful since money cannot buy everything I need. Allow me to return to this point shortly.

Here is another truth we must know regarding the character of God at this juncture: God always acts with purpose. The number *ten*, or a tenth part, is not simply a number God pulled from the air. No. There is meaning and significance to this number.

According to my studies, the number *ten* represents the following in the Bible:

- Completeness of order
- Perfection of divine order
- Nothing is wanting

Even more, the tithe, the tenth part, represents the whole of what is due from man to God. God grants mankind all that mankind has. Mankind, in exchange, brings God the tithe; ten percent of the one hundred percent God has given. Mankind brings to God what is due from mankind to God.

My first thought when considering the concept of the tithe is this: what a great deal! What a great offer! What a great proposition! God gives me everything I have, and He requires ten percent in return? Every sane business person in the western hemisphere would jump at such a deal; give ten percent to ensure the one-hundred percent keeps coming.

I know what some of you are thinking: ten percent does not seem like much when you place it in the previous perspective. However, when you incorporate bills, gas, food, clothes, debt, savings, not to mention unexpected expenses (e.g. home and car repairs), ten percent can be an enormous chunk.

You are correct: ten percent is a significant chunk. Guess what: I'm human. I have processed the debate time and time again. Give or not give. Obey or not obey. However, in the end, I ask myself the following question. What makes me more confident: me giving God ten percent and Him ensuring provision for my life, or me keeping my ten percent and trying to ensure provision on my own? I find the answer to be simple. I would much rather trust the One who has the earth and the wealth of the earth at His disposal to make provision for me. I would much rather give the ten percent He requires and in return live under His infinite blessings for my obedience.

Honor the Lord with your possessions,

And with the firstfruits of all your increase;

So your barns will be filled with plenty,

And your vats will overflow with new wine.

Proverbs 3:9, 10

We will return to the preceding verse later in this book as well to reference an even deeper scriptural meaning to the concept of giving.

As for now, it's okay. I realize some of you have never been taught the command of bringing God the tithe, and this is all new to you. Also, I realize some of you have heard of bringing God the tithe; although, you are unsure regarding the contemporary significance of tithing. Is tithing, in other words, an Old Testament practice or a New Testament practice? Churches did not exist in the Old Testament as they do now, so does God intend for me to give, and, if so, I should give to where? Furthermore, there were other forms of giving in addition to bringing the tithe in the Old Testament, so at which percentage should I start giving and at which percentage should I stop giving?

These are all great questions that deserve great answers. Even if you know little or nothing on the topic of tithing, I pray this chapter and the next will be very beneficial to you. Bottom line: even if the concept of tithing is very foreign or even awkward to you, trust me: you can trust God. When you trust God, He will open your eyes and take you places you never thought possible in your relationship with Him.

Chapter Eleven

How to Enter the Economy of the God Continued: Tithing Questions and Answers

When in doubt regarding an issue in life, what must we do? We must go to the text. We must go to the blueprint. We must go to the documented Word of God. This practice not only pertains to the topic of money and tithing, but we must go to the Bible to find answers to every area of life. Do not run to men or women for explanations; go to the Bible. Thank God for advisors, counselors, and mentors, but anyone who is a true man or woman of God will first turn you to the Word of God for the answers you need.

What better words to read than the words of Jesus regarding this matter?

"Woe to you, scribes and Pharisees, hypocrites! For you pay tithe of mint and anise and cummin, and have neglected the weightier matters of the law: justice and mercy and faith. These you ought to have done, without leaving the others undone."

Matthew 23:23

Question #1: Is bringing the tithe a New Testament principle as well as an Old Testament Principle?

Answer: Yes.

Jesus clearly states in Matthew 23:23--a New Testament scripture by the way--that not only should we be obedient in bringing God the tithe, but we should be obedient in bringing God the tithe with the right frame of heart. The Pharisees (religious leaders of that day) were guilty of focusing too heavily on ritualism and prideful appearance, thus nullifying the spiritual significance and true purpose for the practice of giving. Jesus instructs that the tithe should be obediently brought to God, and brought with the correct frame of heart.

Questions #2: The tithe should be brought where?

Answer: The storehouse, the church.

There was one centralized temple, or storehouse, in the Old Testament. Obviously, Jesus had not yet arrived on the scene. Once He did, and once He completed His mission on earth, gave His life, rose from the grave, and ascended to the Father, the church was born in the New Testament, and the gospel became widespread. Churches began to be birthed everywhere and are to this day. The church is the New Testament version of the Old Testament storehouse. Therefore, your tithe and my tithe should go to the local assembly where God has planted us; the local assembly where God has called us to worship Him and serve others. He plants each of us in an assembly of like-minded believers that we may grow in Him and edify one another.

And let us consider one another in order to stir up love and good works, not forsaking the assembling of ourselves together, as is the manner of some, but exhorting one another, and so much the more as you see the Day approaching.

Hebrews 10:24, 25

Here is my final comment regarding tithing and whether it is an Old Testament or New Testament practice: do not get tripped by this debate. Instead, look at bringing the tithe in the following light. When I bring God the tithe, the tenth part, I am giving Him what I owe Him, and I am inviting His completeness and perfection of divine order into the area of my money; to the point where nothing is lacking, because His blessing will carry to other areas of my life, because His blessing is beyond containment.

If you, in the most basic sense, honor God with your money, God will honor your money. Old Testament, New Testament, one or the other or both, the concept of tithing and honoring God with your money is a blessed opportunity to know financial success. I cannot stress this truth enough: honor God with your money, and God will honor your money.

Question #3 (multiple-part question): There are many different churches out there, thus many different storehouses. Are all storehouses the same? Do I just bring my tithe to any storehouse? Do all storehouses serve as good soil for me in which to plant my money?

Answer: multiple-part answer.

Remember, the nature of God is consistent. The calling of the church is to consistently walk in the nature of God. Therefore, a quality church or storehouse will glorify God and bless others.

I will not lift the importance of one denomination above another. I will not lift the importance of a large church above a small church. I will not lift one popular Christian personality above another. I will not do any of this because the Word of God does not instruct me to do so. Rather, I will place emphasis where the Word of God places emphasis: a quality church will strive to glorify God above all else, above glorifying people or personalities, above glorifying denominations, even above glorifying popular culture. Glorifying God will come absolutely first in a quality storehouse. It is okay to have strong personalities and denominations, all the while being relevant, yet these issues should never overshadow the primary purpose of the church, which is to glorify God. Furthermore, if God is glorified, people will be blessed.

How does a church glorify God? A quality church will minister the true, unadulterated, uncompromised Word of God, the Bible. When the Word of God is ministered in love, truth, and power, God will be glorified and, as a direct result, people will be blessed. Even when preaching is hard to accept because the truth hurts, if the message derives from the written Word of God, the truth will set people free.

"And you shall know the truth, and the truth shall make you free."

John 8:32

Yes, there are innumerable churches all over the world that preach the gospel of Jesus in all types of languages, and to this I state: thank God! Regardless of all these various churches, we are all one church as long as we proclaim that God loves and Jesus saves. We are one unified church in the Holy Spirit. Therefore, it is displeasing to God when we attempt to place more significance on one church as opposed to another church, for we who belong to the living Lord Jesus Christ are all one church.

There is one body and one Spirit, just as you were called in one hope of your calling; one Lord, one faith, one baptism; one God and Father of all, who is above all, and through all, and in you all.

Ephesians 4:4-6

Also, as we read earlier, we are instructed by the Word of God to not forsake the assembling of ourselves together. Thus, it is the desire of God for each one in His kingdom to find a local church where they can worship Him and serve others. Again, an effective storehouse in the kingdom of God will glorify God and bless others. I encourage you: find a church that meets this standard, and wherever God calls you, bring the tithe to God, and God will bring provision to you. Furthermore, your tithe will bring blessings to the storehouse where God has called you to worship. Churches do not necessarily need wealthy donors to survive. Rather, churches need everyone doing their part in bringing the tithe to the storehouse...in good times and in bad. In short, churches need grass-root tithers rather than people who leave because the grass looks greener.

As a side note, I encourage all pastors and leaders of ministries to take a moment and ask yourselves the following question: does the church or ministry I oversee glorify God and bless others? Also, I encourage all those who attend a church to ask yourselves the following question: does the church I attend glorify God and bless others? Better yet, ask this preceding question to God. If the answer is *no*, the time has come to ask God for wisdom regarding what move to make next.

Question #4: What happens when I bring the tithe but I don't immediately receive in return?

Answer: Stay with it.

This issue is most crucial as it pertains to bringing the tithe to the storehouse of God. Some of you brought God the tithe in the past, but you have yet to see the results you desire to see. Here is my counsel to you: stay with it. You must remain consistent. Yes, there will be trying times. Yes, you will have to exercise your faith by giving as you await receiving. Remember, we approach God in faith regarding every situation in life. We approach God in faith for salvation, healing, relationships, and even money. There will be times when you must trust God without witnessing the physical results of trusting Him. Furthermore, if you faint in well doing, that is if you inconsistently adhere to your agreement by sporadically bringing God the tithe, God can only bless you in proportion to your faith; whether consistently or inconsistently. It is not that God is inconsistent; rather, He can only be consistent in proportion to the consistency of your faith.

Then He (Jesus) said to them, "Take heed what you hear. With the same measure you use, it will be measured to you; and to you who hear, more will be given. For whoever has, to him more will be given; but whoever does not have, even what he has will be taken away from him."

Mark 4:24, 25

And let us not be weary in well doing: for in due season we shall reap, if we faint not.

Galatians 6:9 KJV

Remember, if you consistently apply the principles of the economy of God to your money (the earning, managing, and investing thereof), the effects of the economy of God will eventually overtake the effects of the economy of the world for your life, and no one will be able to stop this from taking place.

Question #5: Is tithing really a big deal; meaning, if I do not tithe, will it really be the end of the world?

Answer: not tithing will be harmful to you.

It seems backward, doesn't it? We see people tithe and not prosper, and we see people prosper and not tithe. Remember, we are not striving to be like other people, we are striving to be obedient to God. Also, we are in this race to the end. The only avenue to guaranteed financial prosperity is to have faith in the Word of God and apply the Word of God to your life. I cannot account for how other people prosper. I cannot account for what they have done to prosper. I cannot account for how they live their lives since they have prospered. All I can do is encourage you to choose the road with an absolute destination of prosperity at the end: the Word of God. I can only account for how I got to this point.

The matter of tithing is critical. Let us grasp the severity of this issue by analyzing an early blueprint in the Bible: Cain and Able. These famous brothers carried different professions: Cain, a tiller of the ground; Able, a keeper of sheep. The flaw of human nature reared its head early in the history of mankind when Cain slew his brother. The episode began when God accepted the sacrifice of Able and not the sacrifice of Cain. Whether Cain's offering was inadequate in quality or quantity or whether the quality of Cain's heart was lacking, we don't know. What we know is that, full of jealousy, Cain murdered his brother in the field.

As punishment, Cain became cursed.

And He (God) said, "What have you done? The voice of your brother's blood cries out to Me from the ground. So now you are cursed from the earth, which has opened its mouth to receive your brother's blood from your hand. When you till the ground, it shall no longer yield its strength to you. A fugitive and a vagabond you shall be on the earth."

Genesis 4:10-12

What was the curse? Cain, a tiller of the ground, would no longer experience the strength of the ground; the fruit of his labor. He would no longer know the harvest of the earth despite his best efforts. Furthermore, research of the Hebrew word *cursed* yields an important discovery. We find in Genesis 4:11 that the Hebrew word for *cursed* is *arar*. The word *arar* is used several times in the Bible. Would you believe one place where this word is used is just before the scripture we read earlier in Malachi?

"Will a man rob God?

Yet you have robbed Me!

But you say,

'In what way have we robbed You?'

In tithes and offerings.

You are cursed with a curse,

For you have robbed Me,

Even this whole nation."

Malachi 3:8, 9

The sobering reality is this: when you deny God what He is due, when you deny God the tithe, your money is cursed with a curse. When you deny God the tithe, not only will your money be cursed, but just as the blessing of tithing can spill into other areas of life, the curse of not tithing can spill into other areas of life, as well. Furthermore, what a terribly impotent feeling, knowing, despite your best efforts, despite your commitment to your profession and hard work, you will never see financial success in the field where your talents reside.

I know many of you are like me, and you do not till the ground for a living. The point is we all do something. Think of your career, your profession and imagine never knowing financial success. Despite your best efforts, best intentions, and hard labor, the thought of never profiting is paralyzing. When you deny God the tithe, you are cursed with a curse.

Here is the good news: when you are obedient, when you bring God the tithe, you reverse the curse. There is no curse! When you are obedient to God, His promise to you is He will open the windows of heaven and pour out such a blessing that there will not be room enough to receive it.

I referenced earlier that we would return to Malachi 3:10, and I have stated that if you honor God with your money, God will honor your money. Furthermore, your obedience in bringing God the tithe will cause the blessings of God to spill into other areas of your life. Here is an example of your obedience affecting those other areas. One gift from God that exceeds financial value is the gift of wisdom.

Happy is the man who finds wisdom,

And the man who gains understanding;

For her proceeds are better than the profits of silver,

And her gain than fine gold.

She is more precious than rubies,

And all the things you may desire cannot compare with her.

Proverbs 3:13-15

There are times in my life when I need wisdom desperately. So much so, I would remove my wallet and pay for wisdom if possible. You have probably felt the same way. Friends, when we bring the tithe to the storehouse, God states He will open the *windows* of heaven. When windows are opened, vision improves. When windows are opened, line of sight improves. When windows are opened, situations are seen more clearly for what they are.

Many mornings in years past, I would go to my car and, because of the condensation on my car windows, I would have to roll down the windows to watch for oncoming traffic. Life gets foggy sometimes. The decisions facing us are perplexing. Sometimes we desire to simply bypass the condensation left by the dilemmas of life and roll down the windows, enabling us to see what to do next.

Tithing opens the windows of heaven, not only to pour blessings of money but to pour blessings of wisdom, and if wisdom is to be valued more than money, what should we seek the most?

If you are seeking direction in life, if you are in urgent need of wisdom, I would quickly reflect on whether I faithfully bring God the tithe or not. I am not stating that God is for sale or that you can buy an answer from God. What I am stating is that obedience opens the windows of heaven, and tithing is obedience. God desires to pour out such a blessing on you that there will not be room enough to receive it. This blessing could be monetary or this blessing could be related to another area of your life. In the end, if you are obedient, if you bring the tithe, this blessing--in whatever form--will overrun its banks and there will not be room enough to receive it. I like what my wife pointed out to me one day. In the beginning God created the heavens and the earth. We are all familiar with this beginning scripture of Genesis and the entire Bible. In this scripture, the sovereignty of God is evident over time (in the beginning), space (the heavens), and matter (the earth). With all time, space, and matter at his disposal, God can choose to bless us in any way, shape, or form He chooses. Therefore, the blessing of God in response to your tithe can easily manifest in more than one form, overrunning its banks. God can return a blessing to you in financial form, or God can return a blessing to you in terms of time, or God can return a blessing to you in terms of favor with people, and etc. One fact is for certain: the obedience of your tithe will bring such a blessing that there will not be room enough to receive it, and to that I say, “Bring it on!”

Let me give you a personal testimony to the goodness of God. My wife and I bring the tithe to the storehouse (I am not bragging on us; rather, I am boasting in the faithfulness of God). We can attest that bringing the tithe to God positively affects other areas of our lives. The blessing, in other words, cannot be contained as it overflows its banks. We have two children, and we made an observation recently. Our children do not get ill that often. Sure, our children catch colds just like other children. Sometimes they endure a small stint of sickness during the winter but nothing serious and nothing out of the norm. However, we have known other families that do not bring the tithe, and one common denominator we have noticed among them is the prevalence of sickness. We have not seen these families stricken with terminal diseases, thank God. Yet, we have noticed that these families visit the doctor and even the hospital far more than we do. We do not desire harm or suffering to come to anyone. We simply realize that each time someone sees the doctor or goes to the hospital expenses are involved; significant expenses for some people.

All honor to God: I have never spent a night in a hospital because of medical reasons. I dislocated a finger once, but aside from that I have never broken a bone in my body. Other than staying overnight following the birth of our children, and me staying overnight with her, neither my wife nor I have spent a night in a hospital while facing medical issues. What I am trying to convey is that we are blessed. Not blessed because we are better than anyone else or because God loves us more, because He does not; He loves us all the same. I simply know that we bring the tithe to the storehouse, and what good would it do for us to withhold the tithe from God while spending the same amount of money, if not more, on medical co-pays? I would rather be strong and able while bringing God the tithe than to be sick and tired of being sick and tired.

As we close this chapter on tithing, let me meet you where you are; it is a short trip since I have been there. As I stated earlier, there have been times when I faithfully brought the tithe to God, yet I did not see the results I desired in return. I especially did not see all the immediate results I desired in return; some, but not all. However, when I widen the scope of my view, that is, when I begin to consider my life as a whole since serving God, I concretely find that the blessings of God are very visual and evident everywhere I look. His fingerprints, in other words, are all over my life.

Let us consider these blessings of God. Some of you have never been out of work, and the fact that you have never been out of work has kept a roof over your head. Also, you have used your house to bless others, whether to have them to dinner or to give someone a roof over their head for the night. These are blessings from God.

Your car might not be the best looking hunk of automobile on the block, but that same car keeps getting you to work and getting your kids to school, and they are getting an education. Better yet, that same car is getting your family to church where you can receive the eternal Word of God, and your life is forever changed. These are blessings from God.

You may not have everything you want, but to this point God has given you everything you need. How do I know this? You are reading this book, aren't you? You are alive, aren't you? God has kept you going to this point. It was not you keeping yourself going or keeping yourself alive. Let's be honest: another car should have hit you. That disease should have been the end of you. Those false allegations against you should have landed you in prison. You should have missed the opportunity to get where you are in life. Your mom considered aborting you. Your wife almost left you. Your husband almost neglected you. Your kids should have fallen into the wrong crowd. But instead, you were faithful, and God was faithful. You held onto God, and God held onto you. I am not teaching that you can buy miracles and that God works for money. Absolutely not! Money cannot buy miracles, but obedience can loosen miracles.

"And I will rebuke the devourer for your sakes,

So that he will not destroy the fruit of your ground,

Nor shall the vine fail to bear fruit for you in the field,"

Says the Lord of Hosts.

Malachi 3:11

This is the truth: I cannot prove God to you. Therefore, I cannot prove to you that tithing works. Furthermore, you cannot disprove God to me or disprove that tithing works. You must try it for yourself, and when God proves Himself to be faithful, you must accept His faithfulness and continue in obedience. Again, I cannot prove God to you or that tithing works, but I can unequivocally testify that God is good, that He has never left me nor forsaken me, and that my life before Jesus does not compare to my life once Jesus came into my heart.

I have been young, and now am old;

Yet I have not seen the righteous forsaken,

Nor his descendants begging bread.

He is ever merciful, and lends;

And his descendants are blessed.

Psalm 37:25, 26

Let your conduct be without covetousness; be content with such things as you have. For He Himself has said, "I will never leave you nor forsake you."

Hebrews 13:5

I spoke with someone on the topic of tithing once, and the gentleman put the whole matter in clear perspective. He told me that before he began tithing…his money would literally disappear. He, in fact, had a difficult time keeping track of even where his money went or how it was spent. As the man was sharing his story, the first thought God brought to my mind was this: “the man’s money was being devoured.”

The man continued, explaining that since he began tithing, He seemed to have much better control over his money in general. The result was supernatural. He gave…and received more in return.

If this testimony hits home with you, if you feel as if your money is being devoured and disappearing almost without explanation, I would not let your day end without seriously considering giving God and his law of tithing an opportunity. Do not allow your money to be liquidated any longer. Do not allow your hard-earned resources to be devoured any longer. Take it from me and countless others: bringing God the tithe works.

Case in point: I spoke with another gentleman about the power of bringing the tithe to God. This individual informed me that he brought his ten-percent to God, and guess what God did? God rewarded the man with a ten-percent raise at his place of work. If that isn’t a perfect example of what God can do (that God can do anything), I don’t know what is. The gentleman brought his ten percent, and God rewarded him with a ten-percent raise. Therefore, God put more in that man’s pocket, and the man was able to give more to God since his total income increased, thus his overall giving increased; a win-win situation.

I encourage you: bring the tithe to God and see what happens. You will find that God will provide all that you require to the point where there is not enough room to receive all that He will do; He will bless multiple areas of your life because of your obedience. I encourage you: bring God the tithe and enter the economy of God.

Chapter Twelve

My Story Continued: Bad Decisions...but the God of My Youth

I didn't realize all God had done for me as a child and teen until I willingly stepped from the covering of His blessing. I mentioned in an earlier chapter that the college where my mother worked offered me free tuition. Furthermore, that college had an association with other small colleges that allowed me to attend any number of small schools using the same free-tuition program. Driven by a desire to spread my wings and fly, I left home. First and foremost, God will go with you wherever you go, that is, unless you fail to take Him with you. Leaving home was not the biggest mistake of my life. Rather, leaving God was the biggest mistake of my life.

Remember now your Creator in the days of your youth,

Before the difficult days come,

And the years draw near when you say,

"I have no pleasure in them."

Ecclesiastes 12:1

I did many things of which I am ashamed between the ages of eighteen and twenty-two. Namely, I chose not to live for God. I forsook many truths I was taught as a child, and I came to know the heartache of crossing the boundary into a life of sin. Sin brought me nothing but heaviness, confusion, frustration, and more sin. To this day, I view that season of my life as one giant circle, and, aimlessly, I wandered this circle; never able to get ahead or find worthwhile achievement. Instead, I circled and circled and circled.

Finally, I had enough. I couldn't take it anymore. I decided to return to my First Love, my Creator, the God whose fingerprints were so clearly on my life as a child and teenager. When I did, when I chose to return to Jesus, the most amazing event happened: Jesus took me back. A tremendous heaviness was lifted. I remember taking a deep breath through my tears, and even my breathing felt differently. I had been changed to the very core; changed in my heart and soul. Please understand: there were still many broken pieces littering my path, and there was a massive renovation project needing to take place. However, the paramount problem had been solved: I was saved and covered by the blood of a legitimate savior once again. I could not save myself. Relationships with others could not save me. Even more, money could not save me. Instead, it was God who helped me pick up the pieces of my life.

Granted, I had to endure heartache He never intended for me to endure, but even in the midst of heartache, something extraordinary happened. Yes, I returned to the God of my youth; however, something was different. As much as I thank God for allowing me to be raised in a godly, Christian environment, when I returned to Him as a young adult, it was me who returned...and no one else. What I mean is that I had always served God by faith that my parents knew what they were talking about and what they were teaching me was correct; they did, and it was. However, when I returned to God on my own as a young man, I returned after learning the truth of the Word of God on my own. No, God never desired for me to endure what I endured. However, once I returned to Him of my own freewill, I discovered that God was who He always said He was. But this time, I knew it and experienced it for me. Furthermore, when I repented and returned to Him, never once did I get the feeling that He was holding my past over my head. Never once did I feel He had an *I.O.U.* in His hand to remind me in the future of my past. Never once did I sense God gloatingly proclaiming over me, "I told you so."

Instead, all I felt God saying was, "Tony, you lived and you learned. Now, let's go from here."

So, I went from there. I learned how to get alone with God and pray...for hours. I learned to get alone in His Word and grow in Him. In fact, I was growing every day, and people would even comment on the accelerated rate of my growth in the Lord. I found a church where there was a spirit of praise and worship, and the Word of God was preached without convolution or compromise. Thank you, Pastor Kevin Jerls and First Lady Cynthia Jerls.

Although, even in the midst of this new life I had been given, there was part of me—a voice, if you will, in the back of my head—that continued to tempt me to slow down, to drag my feet, to not get my hopes too high. Why? Because I had failed so miserably in the past. Thus, maybe I was disqualified from sprinting forward in my relationship with God as penalty for years of sin? However, this voice of discouragement did not properly align with the Word of God:

As far as the east is from the west,

So far has He removed our transgressions from us.

Psalm 103:12

Further proof that I had not been disqualified from the blessings of God came soon after, and it came in financial form. I returned home to finish college at the school where my mother worked. Again, I was now living for God, praying, studying the Word of God, attending a Holy Ghost-driven church, giving money to the House of the Lord and, in essence, allowing God to lay a new foundation in my life. I received a call from the college tuition office one day, which seemed odd to me. When I arrived, the tuition rep. informed me that in the midst of transferring from the other college to my current college I had been assessed a fee; a fee that I did not know was even possible to acquire. The fee was for several hundred dollars, and as the woman explained to me how I had obtained this fee, my mind was immediately and wildly trying to find a way to pay this fee.

Nevertheless, before I could worry anymore about this problem, the tuition rep. shared with me that the fee had been waived. Stunned, I thanked her very much, and I left her office and began to walk into the afternoon sunlight. At a loss for words, I remember exactly where I was when the following truth swept across my heart and mind, “Tony, you are qualified.”

Once crossing this enormous hurdle, I continued to live for God, believing Him for an even greater future—to be continued.

Chapter Thirteen

Sowing and Reaping: The Principle

There is a recurring theme in this book: God cares for your money because He cares for you. Furthermore, God cares for every area of your life.

Your life is a field. Some people have prosperous lives and fields. Some people struggle all of their days to have prosperous lives and fields. Again, your life is a field. Bringing God the tithe builds a perimeter around your field, keeping the enemy at bay. When you bring God the tithe, your field is safe because God has preserved your field. When you bring the tithe to God, He builds a perimeter of defense in honor of your obedience around your field.

"And I will rebuke the devourer for your sakes,

So that he will not destroy the fruit of your ground,

Nor shall the vine fail to bear fruit for you in the field,"

Says the Lord of Hosts.

Malachi 3:11

So, you did it. Despite the anguish, pain, and commitment, you brought God the tithe. Good for you! You have, therefore, ensured the perimeter of God around your field. I am very proud of people when they summon the courage to bring the tithe, especially when it has been such a battle to do so.

"What now? Is that it? Am I done?" you might be asking.

No, there is more. Once you bring the tithe and cross that bridge of faith, I encourage you to cross another bridge. Once you bring the tithe and allow God to safely build a perimeter around your field, protecting you from the devourer and pestilence that would try to destroy the fruits of your ground, the time has come to sow seed in your field. Sowing seed represents gifts to God above the tithe (giving offerings).

Unlike the tithe, which has a set percent assigned to it (ten percent), an offering is an amount to be determined on an individual level. More accurately, an offering is an amount to be determined by an individual who seeks God for wisdom regarding what to give.

The big picture regarding tithes and offerings looks like this. You bring God the tithe. God builds a perimeter of protection around your field. Therefore, you, with your money protected, begin to give God offerings above the tithe. Offerings represent seed that is sown in your field. Seeds are planted, grow, and eventually produce a harvest. It is wonderful to have a field; however, you don't just want an empty field for the sake of having a field. Rather, you want to grow a successful harvest in your field.

Some people have never been correctly taught the significance of giving to God. Some think the tithe is the only form of giving. Some think you should only bring the tithe when you have money to spare. Some do not bring the tithe but give sporadic offerings instead.

Again, it is essential to explore the Word of God for answers, thus learning what God desires of us and for us. Once we enter an agreement, contract, partnership, and covenant with God by bringing Him the tithe, He rebukes the devourer and builds a perimeter of protection around our lives, which can be visualized in the form of a field. The field is now safe for planting and growth. The tithe sets the perimeter, but the seed begins the process of germination and maturation within the safe confines of the field. When both elements are implemented, when both tithes and offerings are at work, a harvest is produced; a harvest which is eventually seen, experienced, and enjoyed.

Let us evaluate this topic in another way. We live in a world with various scientific laws or natural laws. Other laws are not natural...rather supernatural. These supernatural laws differ in the fact that you cannot necessarily see these laws at work, yet these laws exist just the same. Furthermore, these supernatural laws are not only at work on supernatural level, but these supernatural laws yield natural results, as well. Furthermore, supernatural law supersedes natural law. Supernatural law dictates to natural law. Supernatural law translates to natural law. Plainly stated: spiritual decisions yield physical results. The law of financially giving and receiving is dictated by supernatural law, and though you will never hear it taught in the science classroom, I assure you, the results are documented.

This chapter focuses on the law of sowing and reaping. Obviously, we think of sowing seed and reaping a harvest in a natural sense. Although this is correct, the Word of God also refers to the law of sowing and reaping in a supernatural sense. The law of supernaturally sowing and reaping is a perfect example of the spiritual preceding and translating to the physical. Let us go to the scriptures.

"While the earth remains,

Seedtime and harvest,

Cold and heat,

Winter and summer,

And day and night

Shall not cease."

Genesis 8:22

To everything there is a season,

A time for every purpose under heaven:

A time to be born,

And a time to die;

A time to plant,

And a time to pluck what is planted.

Ecclesiastes 3:1, 2

"For as the rain comes down, and the snow from heaven,

And do not return there,

But water the earth,

And make it bring forth and bud,

That it may give seed to the sower

And bread to the eater,

So shall My word be that goes forth from My mouth;

It shall not return to Me void,

But it shall accomplish what I please,

And it shall prosper in the thing for which I sent it."

Isaiah 55:10, 11

Then He spoke many things to them in parables, saying: "Behold, a sower went out to sow. And as he sowed, some seed fell by the wayside; and the birds came and devoured them. Some fell on stony places, where they did not have much earth; and they immediately sprang up because they had no depth of earth. But when the sun was up they were scorched, and because they had no root they withered away. And some fell among thorns, and the thorns sprang up and choked them. But others fell on good ground and yielded a crop: some a hundredfold, some sixty, some thirty. He who has ears to hear, let him hear!" And the disciples came and said to Him, "Why do You speak to them in parables?" He answered and said to them, "Because it has been given to you to know the mysteries of the kingdom of heaven, but to them it has not been given. For whoever has, to him more will be given, and he will have abundance; but whoever does not have, even what he has will be taken away from him."

Matthew 13:3-12

Another parable He put forth to them, saying: "The kingdom of heaven is like a mustard seed, which a man took and sowed in his field, which indeed is the least of all the seeds; but when it is grown it is greater than the herbs and becomes a tree, so that the birds of the air come and nest in its branches."

Matthew 13:31, 32

So Jesus said to them, "Because of your unbelief; for assuredly, I say to you, if you have faith as a mustard seed, you will say to this mountain, 'Move from here to there,' and it will move; and nothing will be impossible for you."

Matthew 17:20

And He said, "The kingdom of God is as if a man should scatter seed on the ground, and should sleep by night and rise by day, and the seed should sprout and grow, he himself does not know how. For the earth yields crops by itself: first the blade, then the head, after that the full grain in the head. But when the grain ripens, immediately he puts in the sickle, because the harvest has come."

Mark 4:26-29

"Give, and it will be given to you: good measure, pressed down, shaken together, and running over will be put into your bosom. For with the same measure that you use, it will be measured back to you."

Luke 6:38

But this I say: He who sows sparingly will also reap sparingly, and he who sows bountifully will also reap bountifully. So let each one give as he purposes in his heart, not grudgingly or of necessity; for God loves a cheerful giver.

2 Corinthians 9:6, 7

Do not be deceived, God is not mocked; for whatever a man sows, that he will also reap.

Galatians 6:7

Before I continue to stress the topic of money since this is primarily a financial book, I would be remiss not to comment on an even greater topic at this juncture. During His ministry on earth, Jesus sowed the seeds of His gospel message. Thus, Jesus is the ultimate sower. Many received the good news of Jesus and reaped eternal life; many refused and reaped eternal death. Since the ascension of Jesus, the Holy Spirit continues to sow seed in the hearts of men and women to this day, and, again, some receive and some do not. Yes, this is a book revolving around money; however, the ultimate form of sowing and reaping is receiving the salvation message of Jesus Christ in your heart and living to see the fulfillment of your salvation, which is eternal life.

Now, as I move the discussion back to the financial significance of sowing and reaping, let us pull all the preceding scriptures together and discern the plan of God regarding sowing and reaping. There is a time to plant seed, meaning to sow, and there is a season to reap the harvest once the seed flourishes and grows to maturity. God gives seed to the sower and bread to the eater. Seed must fall on good soil to mature and harvest. A harvest can manifest in increasingly large forms (even thirty, sixty, or one-hundred-fold); however, a harvest is not to be plucked before its time.

Only God, the Lord of the harvest, knows the timetable of the harvest, which is why the contentment of knowing that God is enough sustains you as you wait for the harvest. As I referenced earlier, I have placed intermittent chapters regarding contentment throughout this book. The reason for this, again, is to remind us that regardless of where we are financially, rich or poor, much or little, God is our contentment for the season which we are undergoing, whether in the sowing phase or reaping phase. Just because you have sown seed in good soil does not automatically mean you will see a harvest the very next day. I have experienced fast harvests, and I have experienced slow harvests. As I think on this, the fast harvests have been few and far between. Seed needs to be planted and seed needs time to grow, germinate, and mature. Regardless of how long it takes until you see your harvest, God is your contentment.

"The Lord is my portion," says my soul.

"Therefore, I hope in Him!"

Lamentations 3:24

Remember, the harvest is not Lord. Rather, the Lord of the harvest is Lord (I write this because I have been guilty of falling in love with the thought of the harvest more than my relationship with God). God states that faith the size of a mustard seed can move a mountain, but God never states that the mountain will move immediately. However, God states that the mountain will eventually move, so do not quit exercising your faith before you see the harvest. It is a tragedy when people sow seed then extinguish their own faith before experiencing the harvest. Ironically, this is the period, waiting for the harvest, in which most people surrender their fight and perseverance. Most people know the importance of sowing seed; they simply quit before the harvest.

Let us continue to pull the scriptures together in this chapter. The job of the sower is to sow seed. The job of the sower is not to cause the seed to grow. The job of the sower is not to worry and endure anxiety while trying to cause the seed to grow. No, the job of the sower is to simply sow seed. God causes the seed to grow even when the sower has no idea how God does it. We are to sow seed with the same measure that we would like to receive; give little if you desire to receive little and give much if you desire to receive much. Nevertheless, the Bible teaches us that even the smallest portion of the smallest example of seed, represented by a grain of mustard seed, can move huge mountains when faith is exercised. Finally, we are to give cheerfully to the Lord and to others because, when we give to others in the name of the Lord, we are actually giving to the Lord.

Again, there is a difference between bringing the tithe and bringing an offering to God. The tithe is what is due from mankind to God. The offering is what mankind gives above the tithe. Simply put from a big-picture perspective, when you give God what He requires (the tithe), He will give you what you require. However, when you give God above what He requires (an offering), He will give you above what you require.

The protection found by bringing God the tithe is wonderful. If not for the protection of God, we would be subject to the cruelty of Satan and his evil plans for our lives. Our obedience in bringing the tithe permits God to build a perimeter. However, there is more to the formula than just the tithe. Again, a perimeter of protection around the field is a blessing, but if there is nothing growing in the field, the field is just an empty field; something is missing. Thus, we defeat the purpose. We fail to reach our potential.

Let me pose a question, and please let me pose this question especially to those of you who have been on the church scene for years. I know many people who tithe. You know many people who tithe. They are faithful people, thus the Lord is faithful to them. People that tithe always seem to have just what they need. They have a home, a job, a car to drive to their job, a refrigerator, food in their refrigerator, clothes on their back, shoes on their feet, and every other necessity in life. Please do not misunderstand me. All of the blessings I just listed are marvelous. God is good, God provides, and God is faithful. Furthermore, He is so faithful that He has given to these people in direct proportion to their giving, in direct proportion to their faithfulness, and in direct proportion to their faith; He has measured to them according to what they have measured to Him. These people brought God the tithe, meaning they brought God what He required. Since they brought God what He required, God gave them what they required: lodging, work, transportation, food, clothing, and etc.

Let me take this topic a step farther. Sometimes I witness frustration from people that tithe because they have everything they need, but that's it. There is nothing more than that. There is no surplus from which to draw. There is no abundance. Thank God that they have everything they need; however, there is no room to spare. There is no wiggle room. There is little room to breathe. People that bring the tithe, in essence, often find themselves at the breakeven point financially. Please do not get me wrong: it is much better to be at breakeven than below breakeven. Nevertheless, it can be frustrating when there is no room for error and when everything is paid but nothing is saved. It is especially frustrating when your needs are met, yet there is nothing left to help the needs of others.

Oddly enough, the temptation for those that bring God the tithe and find themselves in this predicament is to blame God. We want to blame God because there is not more than enough. All the while God has done nothing less than keep His agreement. People that tithe bring God what He requires, and God faithfully provides all that they require in return.

Please read these words carefully, I am not discounting or degrading bringing the tithe. Bringing the tithe is a marvelous opportunity afforded us by God. Bringing the tithe is an opportunity to enter an agreement with the God who possesses all the wealth in the world. Bringing the tithe is a marvelous opportunity for those of us that, otherwise, do not have anything going for us; the opportunity to enter a financial agreement with the God who created the heavens and the earth. Apart from bringing the tithe, giving offerings would not be possible. Even if a person tries to sidestep the tithe to expedite the blessings of the offering, it does not work that way. God does not view an offering apart from the tithe as an offering.

Rather, He views this pretentious gift as a partial payment on the tithe. If you skip the ten-percent-tithe and give a five-percent-offering, God looks at you and says, "You still owe another five percent on the tithe."

Therefore, taking in consideration the context of sowing and reaping, we understand there is more to the economy of God than simply bringing the tithe. Again, if bringing God what He requires (the tithe) means He will give us what we require, bringing God above what He requires (the offering) means He will give us above what we require. The offering apart from the tithe is useless. The tithe apart from the offering is wasted potential. The tithe and offering working in obedient unison bring abundance.

The tithe is brought, God builds a perimeter of protection, and the time has come to sow seed in the field. Seed is sown, and we watch the harvest grow in due time. Ultimately, we reap and there is enough of a blessing that we give to God and others from the abundance. When there is an abundance from which to draw, there is more to give to God, enabling us to receive more from Him in return. The situation compounds and compounds, and the lifestyle of giving is a very blessed lifestyle to live.

The concept of sowing and reaping seems simple when placed in the previous terms, yet when it comes to loosening our grip on money, sowing and reaping can be easier said than done. Therefore, let us examine sowing and reaping in this manner.

You are sowing and reaping every day whether you realize it or not. The concept of sowing and reaping is often referenced in financial terms, but the effects of sowing and reaping span to cover a much broader spectrum of our lives. As a matter of fact, sowing and reaping affect our lives as a whole.

Remember the scripture from earlier in this chapter?

"While the earth remains,

Seedtime and harvest,

Cold and heat,

Winter and summer,

And day and night

Shall not cease."

Genesis 8:22

There is a parallel to be acknowledged. As natural seed is being planted throughout the earth, thus yielding natural harvests, as day and night come and go, as seasons change and come and go, so is this process repeating in our lives on a supernatural level. Seasons and opportunities come and go. Opportunities to sow seed engage us, and not only in the area of our money.

You are constantly sowing seed in life. Imagine yourself travelling through life with a bag of seed. This is, in essence, how you live each day. The seed comes in many forms. Yes, your money is seed, but so is your time. How you sow the seed of your time will cause you to reap a harvest. How you sow the seed of your time will cause you to reap either satisfaction or disappointment. How you sow the seed of your time will cause you to reap either joy or pain.

If you sow the seed of your time by laboring diligently, there will be a harvest of reward for your time. If you sow the seed of your time by being lazy and slothful, there will be an unwanted harvest of lack and regret. If you sow the seed of your time in the lives of your loved ones, your spouse, your children, your parents, your siblings, and your friends, there will be a harvest of long-term affection in return. Your loved ones will be there for you in your future time of need if you invest time in their lives while you can. If you neglect your spouse, neglect your children, neglect your friends, and neglect your loved ones, you will awake one morning to find a large gulf between you and them. Furthermore, relationships grow apart over time, day by day, and it is difficult to rebuild in one day what has been neglected over a decade, despite how much you may desire to put these relationships back together. Some relationships reach a point where they are irreparable. God forgives, but sometimes people do not. Whatever you sow, you will reap.

You can sow financial seed, you can sow the seed of your time, and you can also sow the seed of good health. Bad health normally takes root over time. We so often want to lose the pounds in one day that took us a year to accumulate. It does not work that way. If you sow in healthy eating, you will reap a healthy body. If you sow in unhealthy eating, you will reap an unhealthy body.

I can continue to list endless areas of life in which we sow and reap. Nevertheless, I can consolidate all these areas under one larger umbrella of truth: we sow and reap based on the precious opportunities we are given. We are afforded golden opportunities each day: opportunities of time, money, relationships, health, decisions, faith, prayer, and etc. We are inundated with opportunities on a daily basis, and if we sow correctly in these areas of opportunity, we will reap beneficial results. Conversely, if we fail to sow correctly in these areas of opportunities (I don't need to finish this sentence)....

Here is a hard yet productive dose of truth: you are reaping today according to seed that was sown yesterday, last week, last month, last year, last decade, and etc. You are experiencing results today based on actions of your past. Thus, your past and present are either empowering or hindering your future. Choices you have made regarding money, relationships, health, work, and do not forget your relationship with God, have brought you to right here and right now.

The principle of sowing and reaping is stamped all over our lives. It is important to pause and ask ourselves the following: where do we sow the seed of our money? Do we spend money foolishly or on foolish habits? There are addictions other than drugs and alcohol: food, gambling, and cups of coffee at five dollars a shot--all day every day. Do we sow the precious seed of our money selfishly while never taking anyone else into consideration? Do we spend money foolishly by enabling people; people that know better and people that do not lift a finger to help themselves? Thus, all of our hard-earned money cannot go where it is supposed to go.

Furthermore, where do we sow the seed of our time? Do we squander the precious seed of our time by watching television for multiple hours each day? Do we foolishly trade sharing at the dinner table for zero conversation and T.V. trays? Your life is fleeting. There is only so much seed in your bag. I encourage you to begin to sit across from your loved ones at the dinner table. Some of you are fearful, not knowing what you will say to each other because you have lost the art of conversation. Who cares? You must start somewhere. If all you can do is sit across the table and look at one another, at least that is a start. The conversation will return over time. Plus, if you learn to talk of the goodness of God, you will never run short on conversation. God is eternal, and it will take an eternity to speak of all His goodness.

Whatever area of life (whether money, time, relationships, heath, and etc.), what you sow you will reap. This principle is fact and absolute. Take opportunity today to evaluate where you are sowing your precious seed. Ask God to give you wisdom. Ask Him to illuminate where you are sowing your seed and to where you should re-direct your seed. The principle of sowing and reaping is alive in every area of our lives; not just the area of our money.

Chapter Fourteen

Sowing and Reaping: Make Your Requests Known to God

Let us return specifically to the topic of sowing and reaping as it pertains to money, and I will remain on this topic for a while since it is paramount and often neglected. Yes, our potential to bless and be blessed is reached when the tithe and offering work in unison, but here is a distinction of note between the two forms of giving. When you bring God the tithe, God dictates what the tithe will do. God will cause the tithe to...

- Rebuke the devourer (extinguish the attacks that would normally harm your life)
- Build a perimeter of protection around your field
- Provide what you require to live

It is clear that God will dictate what the tithe will do for us, and we are the blessed recipients of His providence. However, when we give the offering above the tithe, God, in His goodness, allows us flexibility and input on the matter. God gives us the opportunity to petition Him regarding the abundance we desire in our lives.

Be anxious for nothing, but in everything by prayer and supplication, with thanksgiving, let your requests be made known to God.

Philippians 4:6

Delight yourself also in the Lord,

And He shall give you the desires of your heart.

Psalm 37:4

Let them shout for joy and be glad,

Who favor my righteous cause;

And let them say continually,

"Let the Lord be magnified,

Who has pleasure in the prosperity of His servant."

Psalm 35:27

Just as we expect provision from God because of the tithe, we can expect abundance from God because of the offering above the tithe. Furthermore, we can sow or measure to God with results in mind. It is okay to attach prayer requests to the seed you sow.

"Give, and it will be given to you: good measure, pressed down, shaken together, and running over will be put into your bosom. For with the same measure that you use, it will be measured back to you."

Luke 6:38

Let me be clear. I am not instructing you to give just to get. I am not teaching you to manipulate God; God cannot and will not be manipulated. I am not stating that God is on duty to perform financial favors and throw money at people. Here is what I am stating: if you are obedient, if you bring God the tithe, if you bring God an offering above the tithe, if you give cheerfully, and if you sow seed in good soil, you certainly can let your requests be made known to God, including your financial requests.

Here are some examples of what I mean. I encourage you: if you are in need of a job, give to the Lord and ask for a job. If you are in need of a home, give to the Lord and ask for a home. If you are in need of an open door, a door only God can open, give to the Lord and ask for the right door to open. Do not give to God just to get. Give to God and trust.

If you desire to be debt free, give to the indebtedness of your church, and let your request be made known to God. If you desire to see your home paid in full, give to the building fund of your church and let your request be made known to God. If you desire to see your bills paid and paid with room to spare, give to your church benevolence fund and let your request be made known to God. Give anonymously to another individual in need if you desire to see an area of your life increase and let your request be made known to God. Give an offering to the bus ministry in your church if you desire a reliable vehicle and let your request be made known to God. Give an offering to the youth group in your church to bless the life of a teenager if you desire for God to show grace on your teenager and let your request be made known to God. If you desire a child of your own, give an offering to the children's or nursery ministry in your church and let your request be made known to God. Remember...

"Give, and it will be given to you: good measure, pressed down, shaken together, and running over will be put into your bosom. For with the same measure that you use, it will be measured back to you."

Luke 6:38

You will find in the budgeting chapter of this book that I am not instructing you to flippantly give all of your money to God and expect Him to wipe away all of your financial responsibilities. No, there is definite responsibility on your part. What I am stating is this: look for ways to give to the Lord above your tithe. Furthermore, as you give to the Lord, let your requests be made known to God.

Please do not get me wrong. Do not throw a penny at someone and expect God to do something great in return. If a penny is all you have, so be it. If your desire to receive is sincere, however, you will give a sincere offering, and you will give faithfully until you see the desired result come to pass. Sow or measure with the same measure you would like to receive.

Again, I am not discounting little if all you have is little. If little is all you have, little coupled with faith is much better than nothing (see the account of the widow who gave in the Book of Mark, chapter 12). My point is to encourage you to give with faith and sincerity according to what you desire to receive from the Lord. Release your offering, pray that God will take your offering to bless His kingdom and bless others, let your request be made known to God...and trust.

Chapter Fifteen

Sowing and Reaping: A Big Bag of Seed Called *Want*

What I am to share with you next was an eye-opener to me. As we are learning about the irreplaceable precept of sowing and reaping, you might feel as if you lack seed to sow, thus you might be disappointed. You might think, "Things are tight. My budget is tight. I don't have much seed, so I shouldn't expect to reap anything in return."

It is true: if someone sows sparingly, they will reap sparingly. If someone sows bountifully, they will reap bountifully. Still, God is so good that--if you feel on the outside looking in financially, yet you still want to get in the game—God has left a backdoor open for you.

"For as the rain comes down, and the snow from heaven,

And do not return there,

But water the earth,

And make it bring forth and bud,

That it may give seed to the sower

And bread to the eater,

So shall My word be that goes forth from My mouth;

It shall not return to Me void,

But is shall accomplish what I please,

And it shall prosper in the thing for which I sent it."

Isaiah 55:10, 11

I referenced this scripture earlier in this book, but there is more to it, which is why I have returned to Isaiah 55. God gives not only bread to the eater, but--back up one step—He gives seed to the sower, as well. Even the seed we desire to sow comes from God. Therefore, we need not live in fear of reaping a harvest based on a deficiency of seed. God is so good and merciful that we can even ask Him for seed to sow.

Let me give you an example. If you are desperate to sow seed to get the financial ball rolling, I challenge you to ask God for seed instead of bread. Instead of asking for ten dollars to spend, ask God for ten dollars to sow. Instead of asking God for ten dollars to bring to your mouth and consume in the form of food (and then it's gone), ask God for ten dollars to sow as seed. Please do not misunderstand my point. If you and your children have no food, and you ask God for food, and He gives it you, by all means feed your family. However, instead of asking for another ten dollars just so you can consume it, why not ask for ten dollars so you can sow it? As we are soon to discover in the next chapter, God often deals in multiplication. Thus, He can do much more with ten dollars than you or I ever could.

Many times in our personal budgets we are looking for *wiggle room*? Bringing the tithe is how you enter the economy of God, but giving offerings above the tithe is how you bring increase. Giving offerings is how you develop *wiggle room* in your budget. The goal is not just to consume everything. The goal is to sow, and when you have the problem of nothing to sow, you can ask God to grant you seed. God is wonderful, and I believe someone reading these words will take this truth to heart and start a great financial testimony out of very little...in the name of Jesus!

Here is my favorite part, and I am not trying to be cute or oversimplified when I write this next portion. If you desire corn, you sow...corn. If you desire wheat, you sow...wheat. If you desire something you want, you sow something...you want.

Trust me: I believe the Word of God when it teaches that whatever measure you use will be measured back to you. However, the Word of God is not restricted to simply money. God can bless the time you give with monetary return, or God can bless the money you give with a return of extra time. God can do anything. Remember, God knows no boundaries regarding space, matter, and time, and He can freely utilize all three components at will. He is God over the natural. Better yet, He is God over the supernatural. Both natural and supernatural laws operate under His authority.

If you need money, but you don't have money to sow, first ask God to give you seed as the sower. Second, ask God for His wisdom if the seed is under your nose without your realization, and this is what came to me one day in my relationship with Jesus. I had a financial desire. I wanted something...but not out of materialistic lust or greed. It was a legitimate monetary desire in my life, and I wanted to see it come to pass. However, I did not have very much money to sow at that time after bringing my tithe and taking care of the rest of my financial responsibilities as the Bible teaches. Then, it hit me. I might not have much if any monetary seed to sow; however, if I *want* something, why can't I sow something else that I *want*? Why can't I reach into my big bag of seed called *want*?

For example, assume I want extra money for better tires for my car. Assume I also want to sit and watch television. I might not have much money, but I have time at my disposal to watch television. Thus, instead of watching television, I can use that same amount of time to cut my neighbors grass with my lawnmower. Therefore, why can't I reach into my big bag of seed called *want* and sow something I want (time) for something else I want (better tires)?

For example, assume I want better clothes to wear on the job to project the professionalism my boss expects. Assume I also want to eat a huge dinner tonight. I might not have much money, but I have the opportunity to fast my dinner and pray for others in need. Therefore, why can't I reach into my big bag of seed called *want* and sow something I want (my dinner) for something else I want (better clothes for work)? By the way, I know what you practically-minded people are thinking right now: why not skip dinner and just buy the clothes? Good for you. We will get to the chapter about saying *yes* and *no* later in this book.

For example, assume I want a loved one of mine to come to know the will of God for their life. I have tried to communicate with them; however, my message has fallen on deaf ears. Assume I also want to spend money on a new phone. I might not be able to convince my loved one that they need Jesus (only the Holy Spirit can do that), but I have the opportunity to give to someone else who has a financial need by maybe buying them a gift card for groceries. Therefore, why can't I reach into my big bag of seed called *want* and sow something I want (money for a new phone) for something else I want (see my loved one find salvation)?

Don't limit what God can do by limiting what you can do. God is God over all space, matter, time, natural law, supernatural law, and etc. If you want something, reach into the big bag of seed God has given you called *want.* If you want something, give something that you want (money, time, sleep, food). If you give or measure something you want, something you want will be given and measured back to you.

"Give, and it will be given to you: good measure, pressed down, shaken together, and running over will be put into your bosom. For with the same measure that you use, it will be measured back to you."

Luke 6:38

We each have a big bag of seed called *want.* Ask God to open your eyes to what is in your bag.

Chapter Sixteen

Sowing and Reaping: The Multiplication Factor

Based on a previous chapter about sowing seed and making your requests known to God, some of you might be pondering the following at this moment: if this is true, and if I desire to live in a debt-free home, and if God will only measure back to me in proportion to what I measure to Him, it will take forever for Him to return to me the amount necessary for a debt-free home.

There is no shortage of good news when it comes to giving to the Lord. One of my favorite facets of giving to and receiving from God is the multiplication factor. When I give an offering to God above my tithe, not only am I eligible to receive according to what I have given, but I am eligible to receive according to the multiplication table of God. This is where our faith greatly comes into play. Remember...

So Jesus said to them, "Because of your unbelief; for assuredly, I say to you, if you have faith as a mustard seed, you will say to this mountain, 'Move from here to there,' and it will move; and nothing will be impossible for you.

Matthew 17:20

Also, remember the power of the seed when sown in good soil:

"But others (other seed) fell on good ground and yielded a crop: some a hundredfold, some sixty, some thirty. He who has ears to hear, let him hear!"

Matthew 13:8, 9

The truth is not one of us deserves what God desires to give. The fact that God has anything to do with us in the first place is amazing.

What is man that You are mindful of him,

And the son of man that You visit him?

Psalm 8:4

The goodness of God is endless. Not only does He offer us eternal life, but He offers blessings that extend to every area of life.

God is God of the impossible. God can take impossible situations and make something miraculous come of them. God can take the little we give and make much. God can take our seed and return a harvest with multiplication.

Just for the sake of using numbers in this explanation: thirty-fold of a $100 offering is $3,000. Sixty-fold of a $100 offering is $6,000. One-hundred-fold of a $100 offering is $10,000. I am not stating that if you give a $100 offering above your tithe that you will receive a $10,000 check in the mail tomorrow. I am simply showing how God can take what you give Him and multiply it. Not to mention, blessings can be returned in non-monetary form. God knows what is best, and God will cause you to receive if you have the courage to give.

Please understand that even though God is in charge of the rate of return, there is responsibility for us to shoulder, as well. As you await your harvest, keep bringing God the tithe, keep bringing God the offering above the tithe, keep giving cheerfully, keep sowing seed in good soil, keep letting your requests be made known to God, and do all of this in faith. Remember, as we read earlier in Hebrews 11:6, without faith it is impossible to please God.

Obviously, as it pertains to receiving with multiplication, the one-hundred-fold rate of return seems best to me. Why not? Why not get one-hundred-fold instead of thirty or sixty-fold? It only makes sense, right?

It makes sense as long as the following criterion is met: the level of your faith must match the level of your expected harvest. If you have the pure faith to believe God for a one-hundred-fold harvest based on the seed you have sown, believe for one-hundred-fold. If, however, your faith is not quite to that level yet, believe God according to the level where your faith currently resides.

Let me share a personal testimony regarding this matter. I began serving God many years ago. I accepted Jesus as my savior. I saw change, and my faith grew. I began to ask the

Holy Spirit to help me understand the Bible. I saw change, and my faith grew. I began to believe God for healing in my body and in the bodies of others. I saw change, and my faith grew. I began to believe God to change my negative thinking. I saw change, and my faith grew. I eventually began to believe God for help regarding my financial situation. I began to bring God the tithe. I saw change, and my faith grew. I began to bring God offerings above the tithe. I saw change, and my faith grew. I began to bring God more offerings above the tithe. I saw change, and my faith grew. I began to bring God offerings, and I attached my prayers to those offerings (I made my requests known to God). I saw change, and my faith grew. I began to bring God offerings while asking God for a double harvest according to my seed. I saw change, and my faith grew. I began to bring God offerings while asking God for a seven-fold harvest according to my seed. I saw change, and my faith grew. I began to bring God offerings while asking God for a ten-fold harvest according to my seed. I saw change, and my faith grew. Yes, I have even brought God offerings while asking God for thirty, sixty, and one-hundred-fold harvests according to the seed I have sown, and, yes, I saw change, and, yes, my faith grew.

My faith needed time to grow. I was not ready to believe for a one-hundred-fold increase on the first try. Maybe you are. If so, awesome! I never discount the level of faith of anyone, especially that of a new Christian who is ready to believe God for anything and everything. As for me, eventually, I made it to that level. Even when my faith finally made it to that level, there was another lesson to be learned: I not only needed faith, but I needed persevering faith. I have found that, typically, smaller harvests come to pass more quickly than larger harvests (it is important to note that this is not an absolute rule, just a typical outcome in my life). Therefore, I needed more than a one-time-faith experience to endure. I needed persevering faith; persevering faith to trust God that He would still bring to pass what He promised even when I did not immediately see the desired result. This biblical premise not only pertains to money, but this premise pertains to every area of life.

Being confident of this very thing, that He who has begun a good work in you will complete it until the day of Jesus Christ.

Philippians 1:6

This chapter gives me the wonderful opportunity to make a point of emphasis regarding a popular scripture in the Bible.

Now to Him who is able to do exceedingly abundantly above all that we ask or think, according to the power that works in us.

Ephesians 3:20

First, I state, "Amen" to this scripture. Next, I desire to understand this scripture in correct context, taking from it what God desires for me.

It is easy to quote certain scriptures from the Bible, especially what I reference as "feel good" scriptures. Ephesians 3:20 is often used along those lines. The words of this scripture, in fact, roll easily from my tongue and lips, "Exceedingly, abundantly, above all that we ask or think." These words feel good, don't they? However, it is imperative that we not stop there. Rather, we must take this scripture in its entirety: "According to the power that works in us."

As I stated earlier, my faith in God has grown over the course of my relationship with Him. There is a greater power of God at work in me today than 10 years ago. He is still the same God. His Son, Jesus, is still the same savior in my heart. However, my relationship with God has been building as has my faith in Him. I trust Him today because He did not fail me yesterday, and He is ready and willing to do more with my future than my past. Therefore, God needs me to believe Him even more than before, even from faith to faith.

For in it the righteousness of God is revealed from faith to faith; as it is written, "The just shall live by faith."

Romans 1:17

Faith must always be in the equation between us and God. I must have faith in Him, and it is according to this faith and power working in me that brings to pass more than I can ask or think. Remember, God is not a cash machine. Yes, God wants to do great exploits in your life, even great financial exploits, but we must first have faith in God and approach these blessings with the right motive: to glorify God and bless others. When this power of God works within us, which is the power of God working through our righteous faith in God, He is able to do more than we can ask or think.

Something humorous happened to me several years ago: I found and married the best woman in the world. The two of us became one. Therefore, I no longer approached my finances alone. Instead, we began approaching our finances together. This was great news because, according to the Word of God, there is great power in agreement.

Jesus stated,

"Again I say to you that if two of you agree on earth concerning anything that they ask, it will be done for them by My Father in heaven. For where two or three are gathered together in My name, I am there in the midst of them."

Matthew 18:19, 20

Two are better than one,

Because they have a good reward for their labor.

Ecclesiastes 4:9

I have learned much from my wife. She is a powerful woman of faith in many areas of life; however, the practice of faith pertaining to sowing and reaping was new to her, so there was a bridge for us to cross. I was ready, based on past experience, to believe God for a one-hundred-fold rate of return on any seed we would sow. My wife, on the other hand, in her faith, was not there yet. Therefore, rather than scolding her lack of faith and strong-arming her to believe for something unattainable in her heart and mind, I simply brought my faith to the level of her faith because the two of us had become one. We found a level where we could agree, and we saw change, and our faith grew. God honors unity over disunity.

Sure, a one-hundred-fold rate of return is better than most, but that rate is unattainable if we are not in agreement. I would rather agree on a thirty, ten, or even double-rate of return and see it come to pass than watch us work against each other; then nothing would come to pass. Married couples: find the level of faith where you can both agree. Use the strength of marriage to unify rather than isolate your levels of faith. Remember, the two of you have become one.

Overall, the process of giving and receiving is a wonderful opportunity, but without faith, without persevering faith, it all becomes just a process. If we are not careful, giving to God can become religious. Let us not have religion with God, let us have relationship with God, even as it pertains to our money.

There is power in the multiplication factor of God, and He wants to surprise us with more than we can ask or think. Begin to seek God regarding the level of faith at work within you, which is His power at work within you. Believe Him. Trust Him. Have faith in God.

Chapter Seventeen

Sowing and Reaping: The Law of the Firstfruits

Regarding the act of sowing, which is the giving of offerings to the Lord, I challenge you to try the following on for size. I enjoy giving a special type of offering known as a firstfruits offering. I know the tithe is often referenced by people as the firstfruits. I agree to a degree. Yes, I believe in giving God the tithe first rather than last, meaning I believe it is wrong to first pay your bills and then give to God if anything remains. Research of the Bible, however, proves there is a separate offering known as the offering of the firstfruits, which is different than the tithe. The distinction between the two is evident based on the differing Hebrew words for *tithes* and *firstfruits*; ma'aser for tithe, and multiple words and root forms for firstfruits; bikkuwr, periy, and re'shiyth.

Let's go to the Word of God:

"And it shall be, when you come into the land which the Lord your God is giving you as an inheritance, and you possess it and dwell in it, that you shall take some of the first of all the produce of the ground, which you shall bring from your land that the Lord your God is giving you, and put it in a basket and go to the place where the Lord your God chooses to make His name abide. 'And now, behold, I have brought the firstfruits of the land which you, O Lord,

have given me.' "Then you shall set it before the Lord your God, and worship before the Lord your God."

Deuteronomy 26:1, 2, 10

Please understand: seldom does God lead me into a new geographical region or relocate me to a new city. The same might be for you. Therefore, you might be asking, "How do I bring God the first produce of the ground if He does not lead me into a new geographical region?" Good question...or even better: "I don't even grow my own produce, God."

Instead of thinking in terms of fruits and vegetables, think of it like this: the firstfruits offering is what I like to give God when entering a significantly *new season* of my life. "The land which the Lord your God is giving you as an inheritance," as stated in Deuteronomy, can also refer to God bringing you into a new season.

There are some doors in life only God can open: a new home, a new vehicle, a new job, a raise at your job, singlehood to marriage, no children to children, and etc. God is good, and He desires to open these doors for His people. These gifts are inheritances to the children of God. Therefore, when God brings me into a new season, I enjoy bringing God a firstfruits offering from that new season.

Why else do I bring God the firstfruits of a new season? The New Testament gives this powerful truth.

For if the firstfruit is holy, the lump is also holy; and if the root is holy, so are the branches.

Romans 11:16

When I bring God the firstfruits after entering a new season, this action is symbolic for a few reasons.

1) I am acknowledging that what I have been given comes from God. What He has given me is a resource (money, car, home), but God is my source. I acknowledge that had He not given me what I have, I would have nothing. This is how we should approach our every possession in life. Remember, “The earth is the Lord’s, and the fullness thereof,” according to Psalm 24:1. Everything we have comes from God. Therefore, it is a small sacrifice, a reasonable sacrifice to give Him the firstfruits of what He has graciously given us.

2) The *first* of something represents the *best* of something. First denotes best, place, priority, chief, choice, and significant. If everything I have comes from God, why would I not honor Him with the best of what I have been given? The firstfruits serve as a reminder to both God and me that I am fully aware of the fact that He is my provider. I give from a place of humbleness, and He receives with trust, knowing that if He gave to me once, and I honored Him, He can give to me again in the future.

3) Here is what I love most regarding the law of firstfruits, and my excitement is completely summarized by the scripture we read earlier.

For if the firstfruit is holy, the lump is also holy; and if the root is holy, so are the branches.

Romans 11:16

When I give the firsfruits of my inheritance to God, I am insuring that the lifespan of my inheritance will be blessed. When I give the firstfruits of my new season to God, I am insuring that the lifespan of my new season will be blessed.

Examples: when I get a raise at my job, which is a new season of income, the initial percentage of that raise, that is, when I receive my raise for the first time, I can give that amount to God as a firstfruits offering. The income increase represents an inheritance, a new land, a new season in which God has brought me. Therefore, by giving Him the firstfruits, the best, the chief, the priority, the choice part, I am insuring that the lifespan of that raise will be blessed. The raise represents the increase, and I bring God the firstfruits of all my increase. It is safe to state that when I honor God with the firstfruits of my raise, that raise will not be my final raise; the lifespan of that raise will be blessed.

When you enter a new or different home or begin to drive a new or different vehicle, pray and seek the Lord for an offering to give that will be a representation of the firstfruits. Your firstfruits offering will insure that the lifespan of that home or vehicle will be blessed.

When you get married, pray and seek the Lord to give an offering that will be a representation of the firstfruits. When you have a child, pray and seek the Lord to give an offering that will be a representation of the firstfruits. You certainly desire for the lifespan of your marriage to be blessed. You certainly desire for the lives of your children to be blessed.

Let me share what I have done when entering a new season of life. I believe in my pastor. I believe He is a man of God. I believe there is an anointing on his life, and when He prays, God hears, and God answers. I know God hears us all and answers us all, but my pastor is called to pray for my soul. His role is that of an under shepherd placed over my life; under shepherd to the Great Shepherd, Jesus Christ. When I have entered a new season in my life, I have asked my pastor to join me and pray over me at the beginning of that new season. He has been there at the beginning of my ministry, my marriage, the birth of my children, the dedication of my children to the Lord, my homes, my vehicles, and I have asked His blessing on these areas of my life. Since he is gracious, and since he desires for me and mine to prosper because the Lord desires for us to prosper, my pastor has always agreed to extend his hand of blessing.

However, I do not allow my pastor to leave empty-handed. I see to it that an offering, an offering representing the firstfruits, is given to loosen the blessing. Please understand, my pastor would pray for me regardless; he is just that type of man. He would pray for me and extend his blessing whether I give him a dime or not. He does not extend his blessing for money because he knows that God is his source, as well. Here is my point: I believe the Bible when it teaches me to give honor to whom honor is due.

Render therefore to all their dues: tribute to whom tribute is due; custom to whom custom; fear to whom fear; honour to whom honour.

Romans 13:7 King James Version

Let the elders who rule well be counted worthy of double honor, especially those who labor in the word and doctrine.

1 Timothy 5:17

Simply put: if I desire the blessing of God on my new season, I need to extend to God the firstfruits of my new season. My point is not to begin a useless theological argument by contesting that the man or woman of God should or should not be given the firstfruits offering (money brought to the Old Testament Temple supported the ministers of the Temple, and money brought to the New Testament church supports the ministers of the church). My point is not to begin a useless theological argument by contesting that all or none of the Old Testament offerings should be obeyed since we now live under the New Testament. My point is this: I have found financial success by giving God from my money in three specific areas:

1) the tithe

2) the firstfruits offering

3) additional offerings

If you feel compelled to follow the pattern of the Old Testament offerings at the appointed times of year, please follow the leading of the Holy Spirit. I participate in special appointed offerings, as well. You can never bring harm to yourself by giving to the Lord when led by the Holy Spirit and the Word of God to do so. Just remember this: you can never give enough to God. He gives it all, and whatever we give to God will never surpass His ability to give to us what we need...and then some.

Give to the Lord. Give to the Lord. Give to the Lord. He will give back to you.

Chapter Eighteen

Sowing and Reaping: It Just Makes Sense

Let me approach the topic of financially sowing and reaping in this fashion. If you had the opportunity to personally speak with a billionaire, what would you ask that billionaire? Consider for a few moments: if you had the opportunity to converse one on one with a billionaire, just you and that billionaire, how would you utilize those precious few moments? Once you humble yourself, and once the lump passes through your throat, you might dare to ask, "What advice would you give someone regarding money." This question, by the way, is a nice substitute for what you really want to ask: "How did you make all that money?"

It's amusing to sit here and speculate on such a conversation; some of you might have goose bumps just thinking of such an opportunity. Just for the record, do you know what I think would be wise to ask a billionaire? "Where do you plant your money so that it reaps the increase you have reaped? Furthermore, can I follow you around for a day and see where you plant your money? Oh, just one more question: since you have such the Midas Touch, and since everything you touch turns to gold, can I please inconvenience you to take some of my money and put it where you put your money? Because if I sow in the good ground where you sow, I will begin to reap like you reap."

Ladies and gentlemen, the earth is the Lord's and the fullness thereof. All creation comes from Him, all people come from Him, and all wealth in the earth comes from Him. The best move you can make is to get your money out of your hands and into the hands of God, planting where He plants, sowing where He sows, and then reaping where He reaps.

"Finally, God, while I'm at it, don't just take my tithe, don't just take my firstfruits, don't just take my offering, but take my heart, my mind, my hands, my feet, my dreams, my energy, and my life. More than my money, God, I give You me."

Then He (Jesus) came to Simon Peter. And Peter said to Him, "Lord, are You washing my feet?" Jesus answered and said to him, "What I am doing you do not understand now, but you will know after this." Peter said to Him, "You shall never wash my feet!" Jesus answered him, "If I do not wash you, you have no part with Me." Simon Peter said to Him, "Lord, not my feet only, but also my hands and my head."

John 13:6-9

Chapter Nineteen

Sowing and Reaping: The Ultimate Form of Sowing and Reaping

It is the highest privilege to be in a relationship with the Almighty God of the universe. Sometimes I almost have to pinch myself. What a blessing; the ultimate blessing. Therefore, with privilege comes responsibility, and it is important to keep my goals in proper perspective, meaning I never try to get so focused on what I desire that I do not leave room for what God desires. Yes, this includes my goals regarding my money.

I value greatly the words of Jesus in the Garden of Gethsemane:

"...Nevertheless not My will, but Yours, be done."

Luke 22:42

If Jesus did it, we should do it. We must always leave room for the will of God above our own, even when it comes to our money; especially when it comes to our money. Where to give, how much to give; we need the counsel of the Holy Ghost to make correct decisions. Remember, our ultimate goal is to glorify God and bless others. We are blessed to be a blessing.

Eventually, you will come to realize that giving to God and others is a lifestyle. It is a wonderful place to be when giving is natural and fluid. Understandably so, it may take time to reach that level where giving is natural, but I assure you that giving is a joyfully marvelous way to live life.

"I have shown you in every way, by laboring like this, that you must support the weak. And remember the words of the Lord Jesus, that He said, 'It is more blessed to give than to receive."

Acts 20:35

The laws of God are so good that when you give, in essence, you are making room to receive more in return.

There is an ultimate direction, destination, and purpose for sowing and reaping, however. In fact, there is a far more serious theme to life than just money, and this truth is highlighted in the following scripture:

He answered and said to them, "Because it has been given to you to know the mysteries of the kingdom of heaven, but to them it has not been given. For whoever has, to him more will

be given, and he will have abundance; but whoever does not have, even what he has will be taken away from him."

Matthew 13:11, 12

It is clear God desires for all people to know His goodness. The display of His goodness begins with His gift of salvation. Jesus came to earth for everyone, that whoever would come to Him would accept His gift of eternal life. Once we enter a relationship with God, further benefits of the Father are to be enjoyed by His children: healing benefits, relationship benefits, and, yes, financial benefits.

Sadly, let us consider the other end of the spectrum. Those who do not enter a relationship with God, those who do not receive His gift of salvation are not entitled to these same benefits. Furthermore, it is not simply a matter of living defeated financially, but it is an entire lifestyle filled with despair. It is a hopeless life where few breaks are given or found. Simply put: life gets better and better with Jesus; life gets worse and worse without Jesus.

You may feel as if life cannot get any worse. You may feel that since you have not caught a break in such a long time that you are due. Friends, when you live outside the will of God, when you are not His child, there are no guarantees. Sure, people prosper who are not Christians. We all know this to be true (I will devote an entire chapter to this fact later in this book). What we fail to realize is that for every rags to riches story of someone who succeeded their way and not God's way, there are a million stories of those whose dreams never made it off the ground.

I am not trying to discourage you with a portrait of despair. Instead, I want you to know the truth. Life will not get better until you commit to God; life will only get worse. The life of the child of God is designed to get better and better as we believe and apply the blueprint for living, the Word of God. The life of everyone else is designed to get worse and worse.

Remember,

"For whoever has, to him more will be given, and he will have abundance; but whoever does not have, even what he has will be taken away from him."

Matthew 13:12

I believe some of you have seen enough. I believe some of you are ready to commit to God right now. I believe some of you have had many opportunities in the past to commit, but for whatever reason you have delayed your decision. Nevertheless, I believe you have been beaten by the punishing waves of life long enough, and you are ready to surrender.

Also, I believe some of you were committed to God faithfully in the past, and then life happened. Disappointments happened. Cruelty happened. Suddenly, God seemed distant, and you felt abandoned. Nevertheless, the greatest abandonment you felt was when you turned and walked the other way. Since then, life has never felt so dubious, so meaningless, and so fearful.

If you are struggling with the weight of sin, regret, dread, even the weight of financial debt, here is the scripture on my heart to share with you at this appointed moment. Jesus says:

"Come to Me, all you who labor and are heavy laden, and I will give you rest. Take My yoke upon you and learn from Me, for I am gentle and lowly in heart, and you will find rest for your souls."

Matthew 11:28, 29

Surrender your life to God. Let Him not only be God: let Him be your Heavenly Father. Ask Jesus to enter your heart, to stay, and reside. Ask Jesus to walk with you through life and to help you make the right decisions. Ask Jesus to save you. Ask Jesus to save you from you. How do you define your greatest enemy? It is the one who stands to cost you the most. It is true for many of you: you are your own worst enemy. I know I was. No one can forfeit your salvation but you. Only you can choose Jesus or deny Him.

Do not be enslaved to harmful decisions any longer. Surrender your life to He who gives abundant life.

It is simple. Just pray, just talk to God and just be transparent. "God, I need you. Forgive me. I repent of my sins. I repent of my bad decisions. Come and fill this empty heart, Jesus. Come and live here. I need to be saved. I need to be saved from myself. I need a savior. So, Jesus, be my savior. Fill my life with your presence, God. Fill my life with your Holy Spirit. Show me how to live as I read Your Word. I receive every good gift you have for me, and I am forever changed. In the name of Jesus, amen."

God has given you eternal life. Receive it. Jesus is the ultimate sower, and He has sown into you. Go and reap.

Chapter Twenty

My Story Continued: Believing, Sowing, Waiting, and Reaping...in an Unexpected Way

I rededicated my life to Jesus in my early to mid-twenties, and I was growing daily. My parents were very kind in allowing me to live with them during this time of transition. I began to view my life from a new standpoint: not so much a standpoint of "what do I want to do with my life?" but "what does God want to do with my life?"

As my focus shifted from thinking about myself all the time to thinking of others, one observation I made was regarding my parents. A combination of age and labor through the years had obviously taken a toll. As I was growing in my relationship with Jesus, I looked at my parents and thought, "They deserve a home to find rest after all they have done for others." I, with that in mind, proposed to my parents that I find a home, and they come live with me.

My parents could see the writing on the wall, as well, and they agreed. However, they put forth one stipulation. They would accept what they considered to be my generous offer if I would allow them to help with the down-payment on my first home. I graciously accepted their generosity in return, and the eager search for my first home began with the down-payment already in my pocket. Looking back, when I consider how God works, had I not offered for my parents to live with me, had I simply left them to fend for themselves while trying to manage a home in their later years, it's fair to surmise that a down-payment would not have been possible for me. However, when we put the needs of others before our own, God blesses us more than if we had not thought of others in the first place.

Even so, there was a wrinkle in the process of looking for a new home; a huge wrinkle. As I considered a new home, I could not get past one hurdle; a huge hurdle. I could not get past the elephant in the room. Remember, since rededicating my life to God, I immersed myself in studying His Word. I found the Bible to be the blueprint for living. Many misunderstand what the Bible is: the Bible is a blueprint. People often see the Bible as a list of *do's and do not's*. Of course, it is. If you do what you are supposed to do when building a building, you will have a great building, a great life. If you refuse to do what you are supposed to do when building a building, you will have missing windows, faulty beams, a poor foundation, a glorified shack; a dissatisfied life. Many turn from the Bible without researching the accuracy of the Bible. Once you believe and apply what the Bible teaches, you will know freedom, healing, and salvation. Instead, many refuse to embrace teaching from the Word of God, not because the Bible is inaccurate or untrue, but because they simply refuse to submit, but I digress.

Back to the huge hurdle I referenced earlier. Regarding the Word of God and my situation, I studied and studied. After reading the Bible, I could not find teaching that instructed me—hold on to your chair--to become indebted for a home, and then, while in the process, pay a lender three times the value of my home over the course of three decades. I could not find this written anywhere. Therefore, I proceeded with the following stipulation between me and God: "God, please help me find the right home, but I only want a home that is debt free."

This is where I lose many people during my testimony. "That is impossible," are the exact words someone spoke to me from across a table. The truth is it takes faith to believe you can own a debt-free home as a young adult. I realize it is easier to believe what you have been told by the majority, which is "everyone gets a mortgage. That's just the way it is."

Believe what you want, but I am stating to you that the main reason why I obtained a debt-free home is because I believed God could do it. Since when do we follow the majority anyway? We follow the Word of God.

So, despite snickers, chuckles, and befuddled looks, I continued to believe God for a debt-free home. Time passed, and in the meantime I gave my tithe and offering to the church I attended—all the while believing for a debt-free home. Guess what? Someone forgot to tell me or I failed to get the memo that there were no debt-free homes on the housing market, and for a long time...nothing happened. Nothing was moving or shaking. Even so, I continued to serve God, go to work, give, and have faith.

I remember the day I walked into a particular home in a suburb of Kansas City. This house was different, meaning it felt differently to me. I viewed many other houses that I considered candidates, but none of them seemed to be the right one. This one, however....

There was a peace as I viewed this home, an absence of anxiety. I remember specifically standing in the kitchen, and while in that kitchen I felt the peace of God. Ironically, it was in the kitchen in our home as a child where I remember feeling the presence of God for the first time. I loved the opportunity before me. The size of the house was great, the potential for an apartment on the lower level for my parents was plausible, and, most of all, the price was a tremendous bargain; the seller very much needed to sell this house. Even so, despite the bargain before me, there was a catch. You guessed it: the home came at a price I could not afford with cash alone. Inevitably, even after a generous down-payment, there would need to be…a mortgage.

I was extremely torn. On one hand, I wanted to believe God for something huge because the Word of God is replete with examples of God performing the impossible. On the other hand, I surveyed the situation before me. It was a great house with great features. It was what we needed. More than anything, I felt a peace in that home when I prayed to God, asking for His wisdom. In the end, I did what I felt was right. After much searching and due diligence, I agreed to buy that home, and, yes, I signed the corresponding mortgage papers with a lending institution. I was not trying to contradict myself or my faith. Rather, Jesus is the Prince of Peace, and I followed the peace in my spirit and signed the papers.

End of story? Not hardly. A peculiar event took place three weeks later. I remember sitting at my friend's home on a Sunday afternoon in early May, watching the NBA playoffs. It was a little annoying that day because the weather service and news broadcast kept interrupting the flow of the game to announce pending severe weather. I grew up in Missouri, so severe weather in the spring was nothing new to me. This storm, however, seemed to pack a foreboding punch.

I got a call from the church where I worked; the building had lost power. So, I drove to the church to check on everyone. The severity of the storm escalated, and we had to move everyone to the safest part of the building. Even more so, heavy rain that day masked a violent tornado that headed west to east. Warnings were going off everywhere; sirens, emergency broadcasts, and etc. I don't know officially how close the tornado came to the church, but it was close.

Soon, the temper of the sky subsided, all looked clear, and then my phone received a call. It was my friend with whom I had watched basketball that afternoon. He asked a question that stopped me dead in my tracks. "Have you heard from your parents?"

I had not. In fact, the last time I had spoken with them they were getting ready to drive to the church themselves; that was an hour ago. My friend proceeded to tell me that the news broadcast was reporting a touchdown in my suburb, and early indications were the area had been hit pretty hard. Furthermore, he informed me of a several-block radius where the damage was most severe—my home was in that radius.

A drive that normally took me ten minutes took me an hour that day. The roads were littered with downed tree limbs and power lines. Cars were at a standstill as far as I could see, attributed to debris and panic; the tornado had ravaged the area. After being rerouted by the police several times, I finally made it to my subdivision. Anxious and frustrated from still sitting in traffic, I jumped from my car after parking three blocks from my home, going on foot from there. More tree limbs obstructed my path. People wandered the neighborhoods with faces of shock and trauma from what just happened here. I remember telling myself, "It's going to get better. It's going to get better." I expected the wreckage and debris to cease before I made it to my home; however, it did not.

I knew the situation was dire when I ultimately made it to my street and had to leap over a huge downed-power line. Finally, I could see my home, and it wasn't good.

The only good news was that my father and mother were there to greet me. They sought refuge during the storm in a basement closet, and God had protected them. As far as the house was concerned, the top of the garage had been peeled like a flimsy aluminum can. A couch I had stored in the garage had been thrown upside down in corner, stacked atop other miscellaneous items and objects. These large items in my garage looked like laundry that had been carelessly thrown in the corner of a room. The rest of the home looked somewhat intact at first glance; however, closer observation revealed deep cracks running along the entire face of the structure. As I walked around the side, a neighbor brought to my attention how the roof had been separated and lifted from the rest of the home from the tornadic force; there were tree branches trapped and protruding where the roof was sat back down on the rest of the structure. Although the overall façade of my home was recognizable, officials from the city would soon arrive to condemn and classify my home as a hazard to collapse.

Before they arrived I stepped inside, and the pool table I bought for an entertainment room had pieces of glass strewn and embedded all along the green felt surface; the front window seemingly exploded from the blast. Upstairs was much the same. Since I was still in the process of settling in my new home, there were clothes on hangers lying on the bed in the guest bedroom, and glass saturated that material, as well.

Any hope of salvaging my new home was quelled when I entered the kitchen; the same kitchen in which I felt such peace to sign the papers. A large portion of the roof was missing, and the rainstorm the next day soaked the inside of the dwelling. Thus, my first-ever home as a new-home buyer was destroyed, lost.

"How could this happen?" If you are asking yourself this question, get in line behind me. Obviously, I asked this question many times. I posed this question not only rhetorically, but I posed this question to God along with other queries. "Why would you bring me here? God, I know you know what tomorrow holds: why would you put me in the line of this storm? This is my new home, my first home! God, this situation makes zero sense."

A state of shock is the best way to describe how I felt for the next week. My parents and I, along with dear friends from our church, salvaged what we could and disposed of the rest. My sentiments were confounded. On one hand, this was my first home. On the other hand, I only lived here for three weeks, so there was not a deep sense of attachment. The home we left had been occupied by new owners; there was no going back. Therefore, I felt caught somewhere in between; a man with no home. All of these ambivalent thoughts were circulating along with the overriding, recurring, primary thought: I can't believe my home was destroyed by a tornado.

Several other homes were damaged or destroyed along the path of the storm. The tornado itself descended, touched down, ascended, and descended over the course of several miles. Many were left to pick up the pieces; pieces of not only their possessions but seemingly their lives.

I thank God for my family who allowed us to stay with them while the dust settled, figuratively and literally. Still perplexed, the insurance reimbursement process began, and God was not finished with me yet. Obviously, I had never owned a home before, and I took much advice from my parents along the way since they had been homeowners for decades. The insurance I had in place was very similar to their insurance (same company, same agent), and I was soon called to a meeting to discuss the next step.

As he began taking me through the replacement and reimbursement process, I was just trying to keep pace. The details were vast, and, of course, this was a first-time experience for me. As you can imagine, I had him repeat several items, but the part I especially had him repeat was the amount I was set to receive for the damages sustained.

Flashback: do you remember me sharing that the home I purchased was a tremendous bargain? Before I purchased the home, the seller needed to sell the house with a sense of urgency. There was nothing wrong with the home; the situation just called for a timely sell. It was not a foreclosure. The price of the home was simply brought low to expedite the process. Also, do you remember me sharing that despite the mortgage I felt a peace about buying this new home? As I tie all of this together, to this day, I am amazed when I reflect on how brilliant God is.

When all was said and done, the insurance company did not simply reimburse me according to what I paid for the home, which was a bargain. No, the insurance company reimbursed me according to the value of the home. Therefore, when I added the equity in my new home in the form of my down payment, plus the sizable increase from what I paid for the home versus what the home was worth, plus my reimbursement for damaged contents, it left me with the largest amount of money I had ever possessed. Include the fact that I chose not to rebuild in the same spot, and that I even sold the lot under my home to someone who wanted to rebuild: what happened next was nothing short of God's intervention in my life.

I travelled a few blocks from the home that was hit by the tornado and found a home for sale that was not damaged by the storm. This home had a downstairs apartment already prepared for my parents with a walkout basement—everything we needed. I liked the other home, however; the basement in the other home was in need of significant renovation, but not this home. Also, despite my loss of contents, this new home was semi-furnished by the previous owners who no longer needed all of their furniture. In the end, given my equity, given the money I had from the entire insurance transaction, and given the selling of my previous lot, you guessed it: I paid for my new home...in cash.

He did it! God did it! God answered my prayer for a debt-free home, and here is the icing on the cake. Even though I signed mortgage papers for the previous home, the fact that the tornado hit that house just three weeks after I signed the papers meant that the initial loan payment was not due for another week. Therefore, I never made a single mortgage payment on the home that was destroyed by the tornado, and I bought my new home with cash.

I emphatically state to anyone who believes your financial situation is impossible:

"For with God nothing will be impossible."

Luke 1:37

As further proof that God is better to us than we can even imagine, little did I know I needed a new home for the wonderful wife and children God was soon to add to my life over the next few years—to be continued.

Chapter Twenty-one

A Lesson in Contentment: The Children of Israel

What I will share next is as important if not more important than anything I have shared to this point. Why so important? All the financial success in the world cannot compare in value to the following: more important than having or not having wealth is having Jesus.

Many of us have prayed to God for financial help at one time or another; help to find a job, afford a car, buy groceries, clothing, and etc. In the meantime, we develop and display dependence on God. We need Him and there is no shame in admitting that fact. It is wonderful to have faith in God and see results. Thus, what happens when you sow seed, you wait patiently, maybe even for years, and then the harvest finally arrives? There is jubilation, celebration, laughter, and even tears of joy. The feeling to trust God for years and finally see the answer come to pass can be indescribable.

So, what happens now? Has God changed? No. He is the same now as He was before the answer came to pass. He was the same while you waited day after day after day, clinging to your faith in Him. The question is not has God changed once you obtain what you desire from Him. The question is...will you change?

It is one thing for God to be everything to you when you have nothing, but it is something else for Him to be everything to you once you have everything. If God is not first in your heart before the harvest, He will not be first in your heart after the harvest. Once the harvest arrives, there will be many temptations, not only regarding your money but regarding your time. Your moral convictions will be tested, as well. Money comes at a cost.

As I read the Old Testament, I find that the children of Israel are perfect examples of how most of us spend our lives. They embarked on a redundant cycle; ever been there? Even with their understanding of the decisions of their forefathers, they still failed to break the recurring theme; a theme of complaining, discontentedness, and sin; again, ever been there?

So they departed from the mountain of the Lord on a journey of three days; and the ark of the covenant of the Lord went before them for the three days' journey, to search out a resting place for them. And the cloud of the Lord was above them by day when they went out from the camp. Now when the people complained, it displeased the Lord; for the Lord heard it, and His anger was aroused. So the fire of the Lord burned among them, and consumed some in the outskirts of the camp. Now the mixed multitude who were among them yielded to intense craving; so the children of Israel also wept again and said: "Who will give us meat to eat? We remember the fish which we ate freely in Egypt, the cucumbers, the melons, the leeks, the onions, and the garlic. But now our whole being is dried up; there is nothing at all except this manna before our eyes." So the Lord said to Moses…"Therefore the Lord will give you meat, and you shall eat. You shall eat, not one day, nor two days, nor five days, nor ten days, nor twenty days, but for a whole month, until it comes out of your nostrils and becomes loathsome to you, because you have despised the Lord who is among you, and have wept before Him, saying, 'Why did we ever come up out of Egypt?'"

Numbers 10:33, 34, 11:1, 4-6, 16, 18-20

Were the children of Israel flawed and discontent? Yes, but are we not often the same? It is easy to chastise the Israelites of the Old Testament because we have the vantage point of viewing their history in a panoramic image. What if we look at our lives in a panoramic image, as well? Would we not see the same cycle? Would we recognize how we sought God fervently for answers, and then once He provided the answers we grew spoiled, comfortable, and complacent?

Once the answer to prayer arrives, we suddenly misplace the urgency to seek God. Instead, we are instantaneously fine on our own; we are too busy enjoying life. Don't get me wrong: God wants you to enjoy life. The problem is we fall in love with the resource while neglecting the source. A haze of self security befalls us, and we approach life as if we do not need God as much as in the past. That is until--you guessed it--another problem arises, another tragedy besets us, or another catastrophe rears its head. Suddenly, we need God all over again out of desperation. Then God answers, and then we slide and grow complacent, and then we are in turmoil, and then we seek Him again, and then He answers again, and then we slide and grow complacent....

If there is a truth to be learned not only from the children of Israel but from our lives, it is this: God is faithful. Thank God for the faithfulness of God.

"If it had not been the Lord who was on our side,"

Let Israel now say—

"If it had not been the Lord who was on our side,

When men rose up against us,

Then they would have swallowed us alive,

When their wrath was kindled against us."

Psalm 124:1-3

When we continually crave more and more to the point where what we have is not enough, something is wrong. We are too easily dissatisfied, discontent, spoiled, and unappreciative. We often allow sufficiency to become insufficient.

Let me point the finger at me before I point at anyone else. I was recently thinking on my relationship with God. There was a time when I was very frustrated, yes, even while serving God; even with Jesus in my heart. I had been praying for a long time to see certain accomplishments come to pass in my life, especially financial accomplishments. I had believed God, sown seed, read the Word of God, sown seed, spoke the promises of God, and did I mention I had sown seed? Yet nothing was happening in the manner in which I thought it should happen, and it certainly was not happening in the timeframe in which I thought it should happen. Money began to dominate my conversation. Every time I spoke to my wife it was regarding money and more money and, "When we get more money…." I was a broken record.

I was very confident that God was going to do something financially significant in our lives. I had seen the promises from the Word of God come to pass in my life years earlier. Once I started experiencing the financial blessings of God, I realized the sky was the limit. I began sowing, and expecting, and praying, and fasting, and speaking for the next wave of harvest to come. However, this time I missed a step along the way: I lost my contentment regarding what I already had. The lost the awe and wonder of what God had already done.

One day, I got ahold of myself. Let me clarify, the Holy Spirit got ahold of me. One day I took a step back. I was thinking on my young daughter at the time and how much I loved her and how I desired the best for her. I have been blessed to learn much from the Word of God in my lifetime, and I began to ask myself this question, "If I could teach my daughter one truth that would benefit her most, what would I teach her?"

My heart was very moved for my daughter at that moment, so I gave the question earnest thought. Finally, I arrived at the following: I could teach my daughter many truths, such as how to pray, how to study the Bible, how to fast, how to choose the right friends, how to choose the right mate, how to manage time, and, yes, even how to manager money. However, despite all these multiple life lessons, I scaled it down to one lesson; the most important one.

"Sweetheart, baby girl, just do this: be in love with God. Be in love with God all the days of your life. Be in love with God regardless of where you are in life. You see, baby, you will find yourself in some undesirable seasons of life. You will not always have everything you want when you want it. You will have to wait for the right break, the right opportunity, the right job, the right car, the right first apartment or home, the right income, and even the right guy. But while you are waiting for all those things that will surely come to pass: be in love with God. Let Him be everything to you…because there is great power and freedom in loving God and being happy…just because.

Just because you have little. Just because you're single. Just because you are an intern. Just because you eat at a five-dollar sub shop. Just because it's Tuesday. Just because the walls are too thin, and the ceilings are too low. You can't go wrong, honey, if you are always in love with God. Be in love with God.

Finally, here is the beautiful side to being in love with God: even when you get that right opportunity, that right break, your first place, and even the perfect guy who will be the love of your life, these blessings will not overtake you and consume you because God is still everything to you. As a matter of fact, all these blessings will be even better because you are already in love with God. You were in love with God before these blessings, and you will still be in love with God after these blessings. Little girl, let me encourage you, just be in love with God."

As my heart was filled with compassion for my daughter, the Lord, being ever merciful, ministered to me. "Tony, that's what you desire for your daughter, and that's what I desire for you: just be in love with Me, Tony; no matter what. Just be in love with Me."

As I reflect on this story, I am reminded of this scripture:

"But seek first the kingdom of God and His righteousness, and all these things shall be added to you."

Matthew 6:33

What I did not realize was--in the midst of all the biblical principles I was earnestly trying to apply to my life--I was viewing God as a meal ticket rather than God. I saw God as a payoff rather than a savior. I saw God as a formula rather than a friend. It was a real *can't see the forest for the trees* moment, and I was consumed by emptying the hands of God rather than seeking His face. I am thankful for the grace of God during the episodes in my life when I have been consumed by my own ignorance. He reminds me that He is my center, He is my purpose, and He is my reason.

If we are faithless,

He remains faithful;

He cannot deny Himself.

2 Timothy 2:13

Friends, while you are awaiting the harvest that will surely come, because the Word of God cannot fail, please, do not fall in the trap of treating God like a meal ticket, a payoff, or a formula. God, the supreme Creator of the universe, the One with all riches at His disposal, the One with all infinite wisdom, if He is content just to be in love with me, why can't I be content just to be in love with Him?

Chapter Twenty-two

Where You Want to Go...You Cannot Get There Alone

It is true: it is a blessing to learn from mistakes. We have all enrolled in the school of hard knocks at one time or another. Sometimes we fail. The key is to fail forward, meaning we must learn from our mistakes and apply these learned lessons to our future. The goal is to not make the same mistake twice. Learning from our mistakes is a blessing; however, there is an even greater blessing to be discovered.

What is better than learning from your mistakes? Learning from the mistakes of others before you make the same mistake.

My wife and I have had the high privilege of working with young adults through the years in the church where we attend; we thoroughly enjoy this age group. The season over eighteen years of age is extremely pivotal. When mistakes and poor judgments are exercised as a child, often these mistakes are made *in pencil.* These mistakes can be erased, often with the help of parents. I realize some mistakes as a child can never be erased, but there are those mistakes that can be erased with dad and mom's checkbook, by staying after school for detention, by working community service, or etc. However, as we get older and enter adulthood, the choices we make carry more weight. The decisions we make become more significant. Furthermore, the ramifications regarding our choices propel far in the future. Some people, for example, get deeply immersed in financial debt in their early twenties and fail to escape for the rest of their lives. These mistakes are no longer made in pencil, but they are made with indelible ink.

Our goal when working with young adults is to give them accurate information based on the Word of God. We lovingly try to explain how to apply the Word of God to every area of their lives, and we encourage them that, if they do this, they will know success much more than failure. Nevertheless, we cannot make decisions for them. There comes a point when my wife and I cannot go with them any farther. The decision is for them alone to make. We will love them either way, but we cannot make the choice for them whether to follow the ways of God or not. All we can do is offer our encouragement, pointing them to the Word of God.

To know wisdom and instruction,

To perceive the words of understanding,

To receive the instruction of wisdom,

Justice, judgment, and equity;

To give prudence to the simple,

To the young man knowledge and discretion—

A wise man will hear and increase learning,

And a man of understanding will attain wise counsel.

Proverbs 1:2-5

I love the previous verse. It teaches that a wise person will hear and increase learning. This means a wise person will continue to hear and that none of us--even the wisest of the wise--knows it all. As a matter of fact, the wiser you are the more willing you are to learn.

When we have been with the young adults, when we have taught them and poured our life experiences in them with the hope that they will make the right decisions, I will not lie: there have been moments of extreme frustration for me.

It frustrates me to see young adults daydreaming, dozing off, failing to capture the magnitude of the moment, and even deflecting all of the information, causing my words to ricochet into oblivion. There comes a time when I want to scream, "Wake up. Don't know if you would just listen to me your life would be a hundred times better? I'm trying to help you live a better life? I LOVE YOU!"

It is around this moment that the Holy Spirit reminds me of when I was that age. I was the king of poor decisions. As a matter of fact, I am thrilled that these young adults are even in church to hear what I have to say because I completely turned from God during that season of my life. They are farther ahead than I was at their age, and I am thankful that they are; I want the best for them.

All of this brings us to this point. We each have the opportunity to learn something new despite how much we know; regardless of our respective ages. We have the opportunity to learn and accept a truth that will stretch us. Just a reminder: stretching is not always comfortable, but stretching is of great benefit to us.

I once sat through a long speech. Haven't we all? It was not the fault of the person speaking. The speaker was presenting a quality speech. The other people around me were riveted. I was guilty of not appreciating the expertise and experiential life lessons of the gentlemen at that moment. As a matter of fact, I sat through the speech thinking of other places I would rather have been. Then, in a moment of clarity, the patience, waiting, and boredom were well worth it when the speaker gave the following revelation. The speaker instructed us to close our eyes and to think of where we want to go in life. The speaker instructed us to capture and determine in our minds the exact future moment when we will know that our lives have become satisfyingly successful; the moment when we will know that "we have arrived."

While we are at this point, let us try this together. Make a determination in your mind and ask yourself: what needs to happen for me to consider my life a success? Whether you make this determination based on money, business accomplishments, personal accomplishments, or relational accomplishments, at what point will you consider your life to be a success? Will it be when you get your college degree, when you get promoted, when you start your own business, when you get married, when you have children, or etc.? Determine in your mind the point when you will consider your life a success.

Next, the speaker knocked me to the ground with the following truth, "The place where you want to go, you cannot get there alone."

It is inevitable: someone at some point in your life will play a vital role in determining your success. As a matter of fact, it has already happened. Someone has already played a vital role in you getting this far. Maybe someone let you stay with them rent free for a while as you got on your feet. Maybe someone helped you with the down payment on your first car, which transported you to your first job. Maybe someone gave you an opportunity to work for them when all you had to offer was unproven potential and scant experience. Maybe someone bought a few extra groceries each week and sent them your way. Maybe someone filtered their closet from time to time and gave you some clothes to wear. Maybe someone left a type of inheritance to you when they died. Maybe someone had little money to offer, yet, whether you knew it or not, they prayed for your safety many times. Maybe they prayed for you to find favor with people many times. Maybe they prayed for you to come to know Jesus many times, and then, finally, you did.

Someone was a blessing to get you where you are today, and someone will be a blessing to get you where you need to go tomorrow. God placed people in your life yesterday to help you. I think you know my next point. God will place people in your life today to help you, as well.

If you desire to become wealthy to live a secluded, self-sufficient lifestyle to the point where you do not have to be bothered by the petty imperfections of people, your motives are extremely off base. You would not be where you are today without the blessings of God working through people. God created us to live in concert with one another. You have gifts and talents I do not have. I have gifts and talents you do not have. God created us to benefit one another.

I know people do not like to admit their weaknesses, limitations, and dependency on others, but for you to be successful...you will need help. I require help to get where I am going. You require help to get where you are going. The formula to success undoubtedly involves another person if not many persons.

Furthermore, you will need God to send you a financier. I know this book pertains to money, but there is more to life than money. Not only will you need a monetary financier, but you will need a *favor* financier. You will need an *opportunity* financier. You will need a *wisdom* financier. You will certainly need a *prayer* financier. The truth is this: no matter what, you will need a financier; you will need someone to help you get where you want to go.

More than a personal financier, you will need the ultimate financier to orchestrate all the details of your life. God is the ultimate financier. He can open doors, close doors, bring favor, lift favor, make the right people intersect, and make the wrong people completely miss. Let me state it for the record: some of the best doors in life are the ones that never open; meaning, at that time of my life, I would have certainly made the wrong choice had I been presented with the wrong opportunity. So, thank you God for all the doors You opened, and thank You for all the doors You sealed shut.

There are doors that must be opened for you to succeed. There are people who must open these doors. Furthermore, there are doors that must be opened for others to succeed.

Yes, you are the person who must open these doors for others, as well. We are all in this boat together.

Place God in control of your life each day. Ask Him for wisdom and leading. Ask Him to order your steps and to direct your path. Ask Him to bring you in contact with those who will bless you and those who you will bless.

The steps of a good man are ordered by the Lord,

And He delights in his way.

Psalm 37:23

Your Word is a lamp to my feet

And a light to my path.

Psalm 119:105

As this chapter draws to a close, do not forget to go back and thank the financiers God has placed in your life. Go back and thank the monetary financiers, the favor financiers, the opportunity financiers, the wisdom financiers, and especially the prayer financiers.

Walk in humbleness today, acknowledging that where you want to go...you cannot get there alone.

"...God resists the proud,

But gives grace to the humble."

James 4:6

Be open to the plan of God that involves other people.

Chapter Twenty-three

Wealth the Right Way

Money seems to cure all problems. Money is a universal language along with the compelling need to have it. Money will get you what you need; essentials such as food, water, clothing, lodging, and etc. I am not going to sit here and write that you do not need money. You do. I do. We all do.

A feast is made for laughter,

And wine makes merry;

But money answers everything.

Ecclesiastes 10:19

The need for money is obvious. The need to do whatever it takes to get money, whether right or wrong, is another issue entirely. The pressure to get money must never cause us to compromise what we know to be right in the sight of God.

As I stated in the previous chapter, I believe it is paramount to learn from people who have been where we are trying to go. We can--by listening and learning--avoid pitfalls that have swallowed people whole along the way. Here is one of the grandest pitfalls of all: money is not everything; God is everything. I know there are times in life when money seems and feels like everything, but I still state it for the record: money is not everything; God is everything. Simply put: do not sell God for money.

It is tremendous satisfaction to follow the ways of God and succeed, realizing there is no need to lie, cheat, and/or steal along the way. This truth is such a blessing to know. I need not swindle anyone, manipulate anyone, or pull the wool over the eyes of anyone to arrive where God is taking me. Rather, I can walk this road of prospering in every area of life while loving God and loving others at all times.

I know, I know, I know. I know it seems easier to operate in converse fashion. There is such pressure to lower the standard and accommodate the quick fix. Even so, I encourage you. I implore you. I challenge you: do not lower the standard. Do not succumb to the pressure of this world. Do not be an instrument of wickedness in the name of wealth. It is absolutely not worth it.

The curse of the Lord is on the house of the wicked;

But He blesses the home of the just.

Proverbs 3:33

Treasures of wickedness profit nothing,

But righteousness delivers from death.

The Lord will not allow the righteous soul to famish,

But He casts away the desire of the wicked.

Proverbs 10:2, 3

The blessing of the Lord makes one rich,

And He adds no sorrow with it.

Proverbs 10:22

By the blessing of the upright the city is exalted,

But it is overthrown by the mouth of the wicked.

Proverbs 11:11

A good man obtains favor from the Lord,

But a man of wicked intentions He will condemn.

Proverbs 12:2

Wealth gained by dishonesty will be diminished,

But he who gathers by labor will increase.

Proverbs 13:11

Evil pursues sinners,

But to the righteous, good shall be repaid.

Proverbs 13:21

The righteous eats to the satisfying of his soul,

But the stomach of the wicked shall be in want.

Proverbs 13:25

In the house of the righteous there is much treasure,

But in the revenue of the wicked is trouble.

Proverbs 15:6

Better to be of a humble spirit with the lowly,

Than to divide the spoil with the proud.

Proverbs 16:19

Better is a dry morsel with quietness,

Than a house full of feasting with strife.

Proverbs 17:1

Getting treasures by a lying tongue

Is the fleeting fantasy of those who seek death.

The violence of the wicked will destroy them,

Because they refuse to do justice.

The way of a guilty man is perverse;

But as for the pure, his work is right.

Proverbs 21:6-8

God demands righteousness in all things, even in how we earn, manage, and invest money.

Furthermore, there is an unspoken truth that few people share or know. Regarding their appearance, those who have money seem to be exceptionally happy; even those who have obtained money corruptly, dishonestly, or illegally. Their facade is one of elation and satisfaction. This is what you see. What you do not see is the guilt behind the scenes. What you do not see is the shame behind the scenes. What you do not see is the anxiety behind the scenes, the worrying, the constant looking over the shoulder, and the constant sickness of the stomach; wondering when the dreaded day will come, when the dreaded notification will arrive, when the dreaded knock at the door will be heard.

The wicked flee when no one pursues,

But the righteous are bold as a lion.

Proverbs 28:1

A good name is to be chosen rather than great riches,

Loving favor rather than silver and gold.

Proverbs 22:1

Whether they admit it or not, many who have obtained their riches by unrighteousness would rather confess and give back the riches in exchange for the lifting of weight from their conscience; the weight of pretense, the weight of deceit, the weight of sin.

Good news: God forgives. He has forgiven me. I remember a time when I was not living for God, and I went on a trip with some friends. I, at the time, was living just for me. I was selfish, manipulative, and beguiling. We all travelled from different parts of the county to meet, and when it came time to leave, we all had different flights at different times. Instead of getting with the one who was in charge of collecting the money for the trip, I simply slipped from sight, caught a ride to the airport, boarded my plane and went home. A few weeks later, my friend contacted me and nonchalantly asked if I had paid my share. I lied. I told him I had and acted as if there must have been some type of mistake.

I am eternally grateful for the forgiveness of God. Subsequent to these events, I asked Jesus to save me, and years later I was thoroughly enjoying my relationship with God when… guess what? The Holy Spirit brought to my remembrance that I had wronged another person for financial gain. It was very difficult, but I could not live with the conviction any longer. I humbled myself and wrote a letter to my friend with money enclosed for my share of the trip. I apologized and told him that I had been dishonest. Honestly, I was ashamed to write the letter; however, two blessings emerged from my obedience to the Lord: it gave me the opportunity to share with my friend how Jesus had changed my life, and a huge burden was immediately lifted from my heart and mind. Only God can take a situation meant for harm and turn it for good.

If you are reading these words and the Holy Spirit is dealing with you to make peace and establish righteousness with someone, please understand that this conviction is a blessing rather than a curse. God wants to make the situation right with you as you make the situation right with others. If you have wronged someone financially, make it right. Give to them what rightfully belongs to them. Maybe you are stewing in turmoil because what you have taken you cannot repay or repair? Still, make it right. Let them know. Maybe the two of you can reach an agreement? Maybe they will forgive your debt altogether? I do not know. What I know is this: when you do what is right in the eyes of God, you will please God. Furthermore, God gives His supernatural favor to those who live pleasing to Him. Trust me: in this world we need the favor of God more than an extra fifty bucks.

Let not mercy and truth forsake you;

Bind them around your neck,

Write them on the tablet of your heart,

And so find favor and high esteem

In the sight of God and man.

Proverbs 3:3, 4

It is okay to seek wealth…just seek wealth the right way.

Chapter Twenty-four

The *Get-rich-quick* Scheme

Not only does pressure exist to get money any way you can...but as fast as you can. We have all heard of the *get-rich-quick* scheme, but this scheme is more prevalent than you may know. It is more than a lottery ticket, sales scam, or shady loophole. The temptation to quickly get rich has confronted us all.

Is God against getting rich? No. God simply wants us to find wealth in the right way and for the right reason. Remember: we are to glorify God, and we are blessed to be a blessing. Therefore, what is the problem with quickly getting rich? Let us, as always, turn to the Word of God for our answers.

An inheritance gained hastily at the beginning

Will not be blessed at the end.

Proverbs 20:21

The plans of the diligent lead surely to plenty,

But those of everyone who is hasty, surely to poverty.

Proverbs 21:5

A faithful man will abound with blessings,

But he who hastens to be rich will not go unpunished.

A man with an evil eye hastens after riches,

And does not consider that poverty will come upon him

Proverbs 28:20, 22

What I have found to be true is this: when riches arrive quickly, they have a tendency to leave quickly. Study the stories of lottery winners and what happens after their winnings come to their possession. You will find many accounts of heartache, tragedy, bankruptcy, divorce, and even death. Why?

Here are a few thoughts:

- Those who earn wealth over time have more of an appreciation of what it takes to get wealth.
- Those who are wealthy but do not earn wealth have less affiliation, obligation, or sense of responsibility attached to their wealth.

- Those who earn money righteously achieve their wealth atop a firm foundation; a stable foundation, even mentally, emotionally, spiritually, and physically (the proper foundation is laid, and the increase has stability to grow atop the firm foundation).
- Those who experience wealth quickly do so atop a faulty foundation; time has been insufficient to learn how to handle money in the face of cravings, addictions, and unsavory associations.

You might think I am covetous of those who have won the lottery or come to large sums of money almost effortlessly. I must express to you: I am not jealous in the least. I must also express that riches gained too quickly or by unrighteousness can do much more harm than good.

I had a very humble upbringing from a financial standpoint. Our home was modest. Our cars were modest through the years, sometimes barely holding together as they shimmied down the road. Our part of town was modest. Our meals were modest; there were many instances of potatoes, bologna, macaroni and cheese, potatoes, peanut butter and Jelly, breakfast substituted at dinner, and did I mention potatoes? As previously stated, my father worked at a cement-manufacturing plant, and my mother cleaned houses. If you are looking for someone with an opulent childhood, please look elsewhere. It has been faith and hard work. I repeat: faith and hard work have brought me to this point in my life.

Even so, with all of these meager details stated for the record, I would not trade my childhood with the childhood of anyone. My parents taught me the love of God and the need for a savior. They loved me the best they could. They took me where they could and when they could. I do not remember everywhere we went or what I received for Christmas every year, but I remember our times together as a family.

A minister shared the following with me before I married my wife. We were in the planning stage of our wedding, and he told me that a year after the wedding people will not necessarily remember the songs at the wedding, the flowers, or the food. What they will remember is how we looked standing together as bride and groom.

It is the same way with my upbringing. I do not remember all the details as much as I remember I was happy, because I loved my father and mother, and they loved me, and we were together, and God was with us.

I have worked hard through the years. God has added to my life since then. I am blessed to live in a country that affords me the opportunity to work hard and chase my dreams. Furthermore, everything I attain along with way is, as I wrote in a previous chapter, icing on the cake. When you do not have much as a child, you come to appreciate the amenities of life that you garner through the years.

My wife is the same way. She did not have much as a child. Even so, we both value the financial blessings all the more as they arrive in our lives to this day, and we also enjoy the following fact: because we were raised without every desire at our every whim, it does not take much to entertain us now. Such a secret may disqualify us from being the most sophisticated couple in the world, but it is the truth. Sure, we enjoy travelling, restaurants, amusements parks, movies, and etc., but we also enjoy sitting on a blanket in the park and talking. We enjoy going on walks with our children. We enjoy a home-cooked meal or grilling on the deck. We might be simple-minded, but it does not take much to entertain us.

Therefore, as my wife and I continue our journey of prospering, as we reap what we have sown in due season, we are not in a hurry to be happy...because we are happy.

For You, Lord, have made me glad through Your work;

I will triumph in the works of Your hands.

Psalm 92:4

There is more to gaining wealth than just gaining wealth. God is infinitely wise. He desires for us not only to have wealth but to be able to handle wealth once we have it. What honor does God receive when He grants us wealth, and yet wealth deters us from Him? What honor does God receive and how does it benefit us if we turn from Him, thus turning from the One who has given us all that we have? How does it benefit us to stop worshiping the source as we worship the resource? Trust me, the best step God can take is to not give us too much before the right time. This is the best step for Him and for us.

I know you desire to be wealthy. I know many of you desire to be wealthy for the right reason: you want to glorify God and be a blessing to others. I know many of you are on the right road to getting there. So, while you are on your way, enjoy the view, take inventory, and count your blessings. Ask God to help you grow and cross every bridge necessary on the road to wealth. Ask Him to help you grow emotionally, mentally, spiritually, and even physically, meaning developing good physical habits. Do not hasten after wealth. Do not be in such a hurry that the thought of wealth consumes you. Do not desire to get rich quickly. Instead, desire to get happy quickly. Desire to get joy quickly. Desire to get peace quickly. Desire to get contentment quickly.

If you are happy before your harvest arrives, you will be happy after your harvest arrives. However, if you are not happy before your harvest arrives....

Chapter Twenty-five

A Lesson in Contentment: The Kings of Israel

Can you discern an emerging theme in the following scriptures?

Then all the tribes of Israel came to David at Hebron and spoke, saying, "Indeed we are your bone and your flesh. Also, in time past, when Saul was king over us, you were the one who led Israel out and brought them in; and the Lord said to you, 'You shall shepherd My people Israel, and be ruler over Israel.'"

2 Samuel 5:1, 2

When the wife of Uriah heard that Uriah her husband was dead, she mourned for her husband. And when her mourning was over, David sent and brought her to his house, and she became his wife and bore him a son. But the thing that David had done displeased the Lord.

2 Samuel 11:26, 27

Then the word of the Lord came to Solomon, saying, "Concerning this temple which you are building, if you walk in My statutes, execute My judgments, keep all My commandments, and walk in them, then I will perform My word with you, which I spoke to your father David. And I will dwell among the children of Israel, and will not forsake My people Israel."

I Kings 6:11-13

For it was so, when Solomon was old, that his wives turned his heart after other gods; and his heart was not loyal to the Lord his God, as was the heart of his father David. Therefore the Lord said to Solomon, "Because you have done this, and have not kept My covenant and My statutes, which I have commanded you, I will surely tear the kingdom away from you and give it to your servant."

I Kings 11:4, 11

Then King Rehoboam consulted the elders who stood before his father Solomon while he still lived, and he said, "How do you advise me to answer these people?" And they spoke to him, saying, "If you will be a servant to these people today, and serve them, and answer them, and speak good words to them, then they will be your servants forever." But he rejected the advice which the elders had given him, and consulted the young men who had grown up with him, who stood before him.

I Kings 12:6-8

Therefore the king (Jeroboam) asked advice, made two calves of gold, and said to the people, "It is too much for you to go up to Jerusalem. Here are your gods, O Israel, which brought you up from the land of Egypt."

I Kings 12:28

In the eighteenth year of King Jeroboam the son of Nebat, Abijam became king over Judah. And he walked in all the sins of his father, which he had done before him; his heart was not loyal to the Lord his God, as was the heart of his father David.

I Kings 15:1, 3

In the twentieth year of Jeroboam king of Israel, Asa became king over Judah. Asa did what was right in the eyes of the Lord, as did his father David.

I Kings 15:9, 11

Now Nadab the son of Jeroboam became king over Israel in the second year of Asa king of Judah, and he reigned over Israel two years. And he did evil in the sight of the Lord, and walked in the way of his father, and in his sin by which he had made Israel sin.

I Kings 15:25, 26

In the third year of Asa king of Judah, Baasha the son of Ahijah became king over all Israel in Tirzah, and reigned twenty-four years. He did evil in the sight of the Lord, and walked in the way of Jeroboam, and in his sin by which he had made Israel sin.

I Kings 15: 33, 34

In the thirty-first year of Asa King of Judah, Omri became king over Israel, and reigned twelve years. Six years he reigned in Tizrah. Omri did evil in the eyes of the Lord, and did worse than all who were before him.

I Kings 16:23, 25

In the thirty-eighth year of Asa king of Judah, Ahab the son of Omri became king over Israel; and Ahab the son of Omri reigned over Israel in Samaria twenty-two years. Now Ahab the son of Omri did evil in the sight of the Lord, more than all who were before him.

I Kings 16:29, 30

Jehoshaphat the son of Asa had become king over Judah in the fourth year of Ahab king of Israel. And he walked in all the ways of his father Asa. He did not turn aside from them, doing what was right in the eyes of the Lord. Nevertheless, the high places were not taken away, for the people offered sacrifices and burned incense on the high places.

I Kings 22:41, 43

Ahaziah the son of Ahab became king over Israel in Samaria in the seventeenth year of Jehoshaphat king of Judah, and reigned two years over Israel. He did evil in the sight of the Lord, and walked in the way of his father and in the way of his mother and in the way of Jeoboam the son of Nebat, who had made Israel sin.

I Kings 22:51, 52

I would like to pose a question? When is enough...enough? Is it not enough to be king? Is it not enough to reach the highest possible position in life and be thankfully content? Is it not enough to live in the temple as royalty? Is it not enough to have servants cater to your every request? Is it not enough to have all the food, land, and wealth you could desire? Is it not enough to walk on your rooftop and be lord over every direction and as far as your eye can see?

The list of kings in this chapter does not include all the kings of Israel, but the recurring theme is evident: the flawed nature and collective discontentedness of these men who seemingly had everything they desired.

Again, I am not here to judge. Rather, I am here to learn and reflect. What if I had been an Old Testament king? How would I have lived? How would my name and deeds be chronicled? How would I be remembered throughout the annals of history? It is easy to assume in retrospect that we would have acted differently in place of these men. However, who's to say? Dangle wealth, power, and prestige in front of people, and who's to say how they would react?

My question is this: I am curious if God was everything to these men before God gave them everything they wanted? Was a relationship with God enough for them...or did they crave more? Was God enough for them, causing them to realize they had been made kings only by His grace, or did they simply forego humbleness in exchange for more power, more wealth, and more women? All of this brings me back to my previous question: when is enough...enough?

Heavenly Father, please be enough for me. Actually God, when I correctly recognize You for who You are, You are more than enough for me. It is not You who needs to change or be educated, but it is me. Be everything to me, God. Help me understand that You are all I will ever need. Help me realize that every good and perfect gift comes from You, that everything good in my life today and everything good that will come later is because of You. Even more so, God, before You display Your faithfulness and grant me the desires of my heart, please be everything to me now, because I want You to be everything to me then. Heavenly Father, I need You more than any blessing in this world. Be everything to me on this side of my financial situation…and be everything to me on the other side…in the name of Jesus. Amen.

Chapter Twenty-six

The Not So Dreaded Budget

There are countless theories pertaining to budgets. Be strict. Don't be so strict. Eliminate all unnecessary spending at once. Eliminate unnecessary spending piece by piece. There are even those who are against budgets. Some people claim budgets do not work. Some do not even condone the use of the word *budget*.

Here is how I interpret the subject of budgeting. A budget is a plan; it is that simple. A budget is a plan regarding how to handle money. There must be a plan if you desire to succeed from a financial standpoint.

Be diligent to know the state of your flocks,

And attend to your herds.

Proverbs 27:23

I believe the winning formula is a good plan with a good person handling the plan; a great budget in the hands of someone foolish will completely deflate the tires of momentum. Also, a budget is only as strong as the income and expense that support it; a budget without income is hopeless as is a budget with uncontrollable spending.

Furthermore, the above scripture applies to more than flocks and herds. Personally, I do not own any flocks or herds. Rather, Proverbs 27:23 refers to our resources, meaning those items placed in our care; income, home, car, clothes, food, and etc. It is our responsibility to know the state of our resources on a continual basis. I do not know if anyone has ever told you this, but you are the CEO over everything you own. You might as well put a sign in your driveway or in front of your parking space at home that reads, “Reserved for the CEO,” because that is you. Your decisions will make or break your financial welfare.

As I referenced earlier, a budget is a plan. Look at it this way:

Budgeting = Planning = Diligence = Blessing

Remember this equation as we proceed. Once you come to grips with your position of financial responsibility, once you grasp the fact that you are CEO over everything God has given you, there are details you must seize and control. Regarding your finances, you must know the following without fail:

- How much money do I have (my beginning balance)?
- What is coming in (income)?
- What is going out (expenses)?
- What is the financial forecast regarding my income and expenses?
- What are my total assets?

- How much savings do I have?
- How much debt do I have?

You must have answers to these questions just as the CEO of a company must have answers to the same questions. Even though some of you became faint at the thought of confronting this list of questions, if you desire to see your situation improve, you must answer these questions honestly and be prepared to do what it takes to change. Yes, whatever it takes.

Let me take it a step farther: not only are you CEO over all that you have, but you oversee—wait for it--your own personal economy. Therefore, if you oversee an individualized economy, here is another poignant question: what is the state of your economy? Did you know that all of our personal economies constitute the collective economy of the nation in which we live? Furthermore, we have little right to complain regarding the state of our national economy if our personal economy, which contributes to the national economy, is in shambles. What do I mean by *in shambles*?

- Higher expenses than income (out of control spending)
- Higher debt than we can pay
- Failure to contribute to the kingdom of God
- Failure to contribute to the needs of others

How hypocritical of us to complain about a poor national economy when all the while we are a direct contribution to the problem!

If you fall under any of the categories just listed (e.g. out of control spending), it is time to reassess your plan and your economy. Please know and please be encouraged: this chapter is not rocket science or brain surgery or brain surgery while travelling through space on a rocket. A budget is a plan; it is as simple as that.

As a child of God who brings God the tithe, I refer to the budget as the other ninety percent. As I stated in the chapter regarding tithing, God is due the first ten percent of all my increase. Since He is the One who affords me one-hundred percent of all that I have, it is my pleasure to give Him the ten percent He is due. Furthermore, I bring the Lord what is rightfully His first, and I emphasize the word *first*. If you try to make room for the tithe at the end of your budget, I promise you, it will not be there. Once I give the Lord what is rightfully His, I am next prepared to manage what remains.

Let us examine our budgets (our plans) in very broad, panoramic terms, and then let us narrow the scope from there. Let us start with income and expense; income, what is earned, and expense, what is spent.

I tend to set a budget for one month at a time. You can have a more frequent plan; a plan for every week or even every day if that helps. Whatever timeframe you choose make certain to stay on top of your budget. Especially in the beginning stages of incorporating a budget, be prepared to revisit your plan with much frequency. Eventually, your goal should be to nearly memorize the areas of your budget.

So, let us begin. What is your income? Whether you get paid weekly, bi-weekly, or monthly, you must know the state of your resources. You must know the amount of your income. I know some of you do not operate on a fixed income rather on a fluctuating income. If you are in this category, you must still determine a reliable amount of income, using history as a guide. If you must, take your worst-case scenario to cover all possible angles. Once you set aside the tithe based on ten-percent of your income (remember that the tithe builds a safe perimeter around your field), the next step is to determine your remaining priorities.

What are your expenses? Let us keep this very simple. What are the basic, most important financial concerns in your life?

- Food
- Clothes
- Lodging (a place to live)
- Transportation (depending on where you live)
- Medical/Life Insurance

The need for food and clothing are simple to understand. Everyone needs a home, as well. Furthermore, we need items and utilities within the home to make the home habitable, such as water and electricity. Many people drive to work, and work is the primary source of income for their lives; thus, transportation is an essential expense. We know not what tomorrow holds, which is why it is wise to have both medical and life insurance. Expenses such as these are fixed expenses, meaning these expenses are first and foremost, meaning these expenses are rigid and permit little if any flexibility. Even so, even after admitting that there is no way around certain fixes expenses in life, we must always make room for discretion.

Discretion can be interpreted as freedom of judgment or choice. The Bible, in fact, speaks to discretion:

Discretion will preserve you;

Understanding will keep you.

Proverbs 2:11

My son, let them not depart from your eyes—

Keep sound wisdom and discretion.

Proverbs 3:21

My son, pay attention to my wisdom;

Lend your ear to my understanding,

That you may preserve discretion,

And your lips may keep knowledge.

Proverbs 5:1, 2

Even God leads us by example in the use of discretion:

He has made the earth by His power,

He has established the world by His wisdom,

And has stretched out the heavens at His discretion.

Jeremiah 10:12

Case in point: I enjoy the restaurants in Kansas City; several immediately rush to mind. However, there have been times in my life when frequenting these restaurants was not a responsible decision to make. There have been times when choosing to eat at home instead of eating out was executing discretion. Much the same, there have been times when choosing modest, affordable clothing was the best way to go instead of choosing the latest designer apparel that just came off the line. What have I done in these cases? I used discretion. I was under control. I was cognizant of the situation. Based on your income, you may need to dial down your eating habits to allow for the greater good of your financial welfare.

A home or living space, on the other hand, is a more concrete expense from month to month. Nevertheless, you can still apply the same modest approach to lodging. You will be best served to choose lodging that is in your price range versus choosing a home or apartment that will be a continual financial burden every month. Please do not choose homes, apartments, cars, clothes, and even restaurants based on appearance or pride. The appearance you desire to portray will only last for a short time as heartache moves into position around the corner.

Pride goes before destruction,

And a haughty spirit before a fall.

Proverbs 16:18

All of your financial decisions must be based on what you can afford, not based on how much you can charge or borrow. Stay with concrete facts and numbers. Know your income and do your best to stay within your income.

Start with the essential items in life:

- What is your income?

Now begin to subtract from there:

- What is ten percent of your income (the tithe that is due God)?
- How much is your house payment or rent?
- How much are the utilities within your home (electric, gas, water, trash, and etc.)?
- How much is your car or transportation payment?
- How much is the gasoline cost for your transportation?

- How much do you need to spend on food?
- How much do you need to spend on clothes?
- How much do you allocate toward paying your debts?
- How much do you allocate toward savings?
- Is there anything left to give as an offering; sowing seed toward a future harvest?

Here is how I approach setting a plan or budget. I do not believe in a universal budget across the board for everyone. We have different lives with different details; some are married, some are single, some have children, some do not have children, some drive a great distance to work, some walk, some work at home, some require medication, some do not, and etc. I do not believe one plan or budget covers the financial needs of everyone, rather I believe everyone needs a plan. Instead, I believe in universal principles; principles from the Word of God. Although we are different with different situations, the principles are the same for all of us (e.g. spend responsibility within your means, and then sacrifice and work to get to the next level).

Jesus admonished:

"For which of you, intending to build a tower, does not sit down first and count the cost, whether he has enough to finish it—lest, after he has laid the foundation, and is not able to finish, all who see it begin to mock him, saying, 'This man began to build and was not able to finish.'"

Luke 14:28-30

Always keep in mind that God is as practical as He is miraculous. The same God of faith is the same God of wisdom.

We have reached the crux of the matter; where decisions must be made. How much money do you have and what can you afford? This principal principle applies to us all. Furthermore, this principle does not only apply to the poor since those who have more money often have more expenses. Wealth is not simply what you make. Instead, wealth is what you keep when all else is paid.

I remember when I first began working in the accounting department of the church where I attend. I thought if our church could just get to a certain level of income each week, we would have it made forever. As the years passed and the income grew, the expenses correspondingly grew. Yes, more people attending the church meant more church income; however, more people attending the church meant more staff members necessary to manage the growth, which meant more payroll expense, which meant more payroll taxes, which meant more health insurance expense. More people on Sunday meant more activities through the week, which meant more electricity, gas, and utilities through the week. More people meant more printing, postage, and even more paper towels and toilet tissue in the restrooms.

All of us--poor and rich alike--must abide by the universal principle of living within our means.

Living within our means challenges us to be creative regarding our expenses, such as…

- Live in a place that is adequately sized yet affordable
- Consistently eat food that is sufficient yet not wastefully exorbitant
- Wear clothes that serve purpose, not serve pride
- Drive a vehicle that is affordable…even carpool or ride public transportation if need be

Again, I believe in flexibility from one budget to the next. One person might have a large family, and yet they live within walking distance to work or use public transportation. Therefore, a person such as this might spend more money on the square-footage of their home rather than on a second car. Another person might be single and spend less on square-footage, food, and clothing as opposed to a family, and yet this single person might be taking night classes, which costs tuition. The point is this: know your income and contour your expenses to your income. Taking this step is more than half the battle when it comes to a successful budget.

Chapter Twenty-seven

The No So Dreaded Budget Continues: God Is As Practical As He Is Miraculous

As we continue the topic of constructing a budget, meaning constructing a financial plan, please keep in mind that God is as practical as He is miraculous. The same God of faith is the same God of wisdom.

Keeping this truth in mind, here are some examples of how budgets can appear on paper:

Example Budget # 1 (standard)

- Income (add)
- Tithe (subtract)
- Offering (subtract)
- Mortgage/Rent &Utilities (subtract)
- Car Payment & Gasoline (subtract)
- Medical/life insurance (subtract)
- Groceries/Clothing (subtract)
- Debt (subtract)
- Savings (subtract)
- Discretionary Spending: luxuries after necessities (subtract)

Example Budget # 2 (someone with small children to feed)

- Income (add)
- Tithe (subtract)
- Mortgage/Rent &Utilities (subtract)
- Groceries/Clothing (subtract)
- Car Payment & Gasoline (subtract)
- Medical/life Insurance (subtract)
- Debt (subtract)
- Savings (subtract)
- Offering (subtract)
- Discretionary Spending: luxuries after necessities (subtract)

Example Budget # 3 (someone who owns their car)

- Income (add)
- Tithe (subtract)
- Offering (subtract)
- Mortgage/Rent &Utilities (subtract)
- Groceries/Clothing (subtract)
- Medical/life Insurance (subtract)

- Gasoline (subtract)
- Debt (subtract)
- Savings (subtract)
- Discretionary Spending: luxuries after necessities (subtract)

Example Budget # 4 (someone who owns their home and cars)

- Income (add)
- Tithe (subtract)
- Offering (subtract)
- Groceries/Clothing (subtract)
- Medical/life Insurance (subtract)
- Debt…if any (subtract)
- Savings (subtract)
- Discretionary Spending: luxuries after necessities (subtract)

Example Budget # 5 (a young adult living at home with no debt while attending college)

- Income (add)
- Tithe (subtract)
- Offering (subtract)
- Medical Insurance if not on parent's plan (subtract)

- Tuition and Books (subtract)
- Groceries/Clothing (subtract)
- Savings (subtract)
- Discretionary Spending: luxuries after necessities (subtract)

Here are a few points of clarification. Yes, the previous examples are flexible from one to the other; however, there are some staples that never change.

- Establish your income at the outset (do not start spending until you do)
- The tithe is first (honor God with ten percent, and He will continue to honor you with one-hundred percent)
- Remember the offering (the tithe is essential to what you need, the offering is essential to above what you need)
- Debt is your responsibility to pay until it is gone (chapter on debt upcoming)
- Savings and bracing for the future is paramount (chapter on savings upcoming)
- Discretionary spending is always listed last (necessities always before luxuries)

Those of you who have an astute eye may have caught an anomaly within the preceding sample budgets. You may have noticed that, even though the tithe was listed as high priority without fail, I did maneuver the location of offerings a little...and here is why.

The fact that I maneuvered offerings in no way diminishes the role of offerings in our finances. However, I relocated offerings because until we get on top of our expenses rather than our expenses being on top of us, meaning the financial obligations that have worked their way into our lives, we must honor the previous financial obligations we have made.

Better not to vow than to vow and not pay.

Ecclesiastes 5:5

In other words, the water company will not put off what you owe while you give offerings to your church; so, don't try it. Again, this does not erase the need to give offerings from the equation. Remember, the tithe establishes a safe perimeter around the field as God rebukes the devourer, and the seed (the offerings) are sown in the field to bring increase. What this means is we may have to get creative when it comes to sowing seed. I mentioned in the chapters on sowing and reaping that God not only gives bread to the eater but seed to the sower. Once you factor your income, bring the tithe to God, and then once you pay expenses from previous financial obligations, there may not be much of anything left. Still, you can determine at this point what you are able to give as an offering. Remember, offerings also bring wiggle room. Therefore, if you have to give offerings in the form of cash as you forego a meal or in the form of time by donating labor to your church or others, continue to find ways to sow seed by all means. Once you get more on top of your expenses by using discretion, thus slashing expenses as much as possible, the good news is there eventually will be more left to give as offerings.

Also on the topic of budgets, I know there are financial experts who will instruct you to pay yourself first with your income. I disagree. Many of you are in your current financial position because you have been paying yourself first. So, why are things not better if you have been paying yourself first? Others may instruct you to pay your taxes first and then pay your tithe after you have paid the government. I believe a true child of God will not cheat God or the government. Pay your taxes, just make certain to pay God; there is no income to tax if not for God providing one-hundred percent of the income. Pay God first and by doing so you are placing Him in charge of the rest of your finances.

And Jesus answered and said to them, "Render to Caesar the things that are Caesar's, and to God the things that are God's." And they marveled at Him.

Mark 12:17

Again, I know there are financial experts who will instruct you that budgets, in general, do not work. Call it a budget if you want or don't want. However, there must be a plan in place to succeed financially. You plan for the success of your career. You plan for the success of your family. You even plan for your next vacation. There must be a plan in place for you to succeed financially.

Where there is no vision, the people perish: but he that keepeth the law, happy is he.

Proverbs 29:18 KJV

Here are some other ideas to help save money or use money more efficiently. Hopefully some of these ideas will be of assistance to you.

- If you have no idea where your money is going, run an audit on yourself (keep receipts for a month to track all expenditures for an accurate picture)
- Pay by cash, check, or debit/check cards in all that you do (old saying: you cannot spend what you do not have)
- Pay bills and necessities as soon as you get money in your possession (our thinking tends to change the longer we have money, increasing our tendency to spend it elsewhere)
- Attempt to operate your monthly budget using a typical four-week system, which means once a quarter you will have a fifth week of extra income, which will assist you with some of those pesky periodic expenses in life
- Determine how much money you can spend on debt each month and spend at least that amount every month until all your debts are paid (do not lessen this amount toward debt until all debts are paid; there is more on debt in an upcoming chapter)
- Attempt to pay an extra house payment each year (this will decrease the overall number of years on your mortgage)

- Attempt to pay extra on your automobile(s) and pay it (them) off before the end of the five-year lease (cars can depreciate much in five years)
- Downsize to a smaller home if need be
- Downsize to one car if need be
- Cut one dinner-out per week
- Cook at home as much as possible
- Stretch your dollar by cooking dinner at home at night and using the leftovers for lunch the next day (try not to waste anything, especially food)
- Shop at the grocery store with several meals in mind at once (make a list, take cash, and stick to your list and your cash)
- Begin carpooling or biking to work or school
- Cut cable television from your budget or at least trim your cable package by eliminating unnecessary channels
- Designate a coin jar for loose change and put it to use at the end of every month for a designated purpose
- Check thrift or second-hand stores before you buy elsewhere at full price for clothing
- Check grocery stores where you know prices are lower
- Experiment with off-brand items when purchasing groceries (this may not work every time, but you will most likely find sufficient replacements to certain foods at lower costs)
- Use coupons when shopping for groceries and other items

- Use coupons and then set aside the amount of money you save using coupons in a designated place to be put to a specific use later
- Use hand towels where possible instead of paper towels
- Run errands efficiently (run daily and weekly errands on one circuit, thus saving on gasoline rather than running several separate errands)
- Know checking and saving account balances at all times to avoid overdraft charges
- Do not speed or park illegally (a monthly budget can be wrecked by a ticket or an insurance increase)
- Do your own house cleaning and yard work
- Sell anything around the house you no longer need and wisely apply the profits

Some of the preceding ideas may seem oversimplified and even humorous. Still, the variables and possibilities within personal budgets are endless, and it is worth considering all of them until you find what works best for you. The principle remains the same: we must learn to live within our means.

We might as well resolve the following issue before we continue. If you desire to wisely manage your money, you must learn to say *no* and say *no* often. If you follow your impulses at every turn, life will not get better but worse.

Here is another tough truth when you first try to walk in financial balance: it will seem that more factors in life are against you than for you. You will have to prevail against a cruel world, a selfish world, an unforgiving world, the disadvantage of your current financial state, the disadvantage of the poor choices you have already made, and the list is plentiful.

Nevertheless, here is the overriding factor that you have in your corner.

"For with God nothing will be impossible."

Luke 1:37

Therefore,

Ye are of God, little children, and have overcome them: because greater is he that is in you, than he that is in the world.

1 John 4:4 KJV

I am not stating that living by a budget is easy, but, in the name of Jesus, you can do it.

I am not stating that everyone is going to give you a break, but, in the name of Jesus, you can do it.

I am not stating that every detail is going to fall perfectly in place, but, in the name of Jesus, you can do it.

I am not stating that there will be an absence of setbacks, but, in the name of Jesus, you can do it.

I am not stating everything will materialize as soon as you desire, but, in the name of Jesus, you can do it.

Finally, when it all gets to be too much, when it feels as if there is too much to consider and process and you simply need to take a break, I encourage you to escape into the following words of Jesus.

"Therefore I say to you, do not worry about your life, what you will eat or what you will drink; nor about your body, what you will put on. Is not life more than food and the body more than clothing? Look at the birds of the air, for they neither sow nor reap nor gather into barns; yet your heavenly Father feeds them. Are you not of more value than they? Which of you by worrying can add one cubit to his stature? So why do you worry about clothing? Consider the lilies of the field, how they grow: they neither toil nor spin; and yet I say to you that even Solomon in all his glory was not arrayed like one of these. Now if God so clothes the grass of the field, which today is, and tomorrow is thrown into the oven, will He not much more clothe you, O you of little faith? Therefore, do not worry, saying, 'What shall we eat?' or 'What shall we drink?' or 'What shall we wear?' For after all these things the Gentiles seek. For your heavenly Father knows that you need all these things. But seek first the kingdom of God and His righteousness, and all these things shall be added to you. Therefore do not worry about tomorrow, for tomorrow will worry about its own things. Sufficient for the day is its own trouble."

Matthew 6:25-34

When all is said and done, when you are a child of God, the ultimate responsibility of provision belongs to God. The Bible teaches us that apart from Jesus we can do nothing. Ultimately, it is up to God to care for His children much like we care for our children. My children do not awake in the morning and fret over income, the next meal, clothes for that day, or anything of the like. No, they awake resting comfortably in the fact that daddy and mommy have it all worked out.

It is the same between us and God. Sure, you can labor to buy food, but you cannot create food. Sure, you can labor to buy clothes, but you cannot create the material to design clothes. Sure, you can labor to pay a mortgage, but you cannot create the building materials to build a home.

Let us do all we can do and let God do the rest. The moment we fail to do what we can or the moment we try to do God's job for Him, we are out of commission.

The budget examples in this chapter are merely those: examples. The point of this chapter is to accentuate that the dreaded budget does not have to be so dreaded. A budget is a plan; pure and simple. Pray and ask God for wisdom. He will help you formulate and navigate a plan. Be accountable to someone regarding your budget if need be. I guarantee you, once you walk through your budget a few times, it will become a not so dreaded experience. In fact, I dare state that it will become an empowering experience. You must start a plan to have any financial success in your life. Be encouraged: if you include Him, God will be with you.

Chapter Twenty-eight

No Way around Discipline

Obviously, I would not care much for you if I lied to you. There is no way around discipline if you desire to be financially successful. I know there are those who spend wealth wildly, seemingly with impunity. Still, we should not model ourselves after such people. Our goal is not to model after people but model after the Word of God. Faith and hard work; please keep these words at the forefront for the rest of your life.

Discipline is an intriguing word. Many people want discipline; although, few are willing to walk the road of discipline. Discipline is easy to want yet difficult to attain. Discipline is the difference between setting a goal and achieving an accomplishment. Discipline is the chasm between constructing a financial plan and living the plan. Anyone can construct a plan, but it takes a person of discipline to execute a plan.

Whoever has no rule over his own spirit

Is like a city broken down, without walls.

Proverbs 25:28

You must have discipline to be financially successful; not only in obtaining wealth but in handling wealth once you obtain it. Self-control is essential in preventing poor decisions.

But the fruit of the Spirit is love, joy, peace, longsuffering, kindness, goodness, faithfulness, gentleness, self-control. Against such there is no law.

Galatians 5:22, 23

I have heard opinions as to why self-control is listed last regarding the fruit of the Spirit. Some believe it is listed last because it is the most difficult to achieve. I understand that conjecture. Self-control is a quality that has often eluded me. Self-control is necessary when we speak, look, listen, and act in general. Money, food, words, actions, and etc., all of these are governed by the presence or absence of self-control. I cannot express to you how many times I have constructed an eating and exercise plan only to fall miserably short in accomplishing my goal. If you would like to admit this truth and join me in this boat, there is plenty of room.

Even so, when analyzing a tough subject such as discipline, I am not one to promote condemnation.

There is therefore now no condemnation to those who are in Christ Jesus, who do not walk according to the flesh, but according to the Spirit.

Romans 8:1

Yes, there have been instances when I have set goals and fallen short. However, I, in the midst of striving for such goals, accomplished more than I would have had I not set a goal in the first place. There is an expression that registers with me: “Shoot for the moon. If you fail, you will still be among the stars,” meaning something is better than nothing.

I know some of you take a more hardline approach. If you are able to set up a goal and knock it down every time, I applaud you. However, keeping the rest of us in mind, maybe you desire to lose thirty pounds yet only lose twenty. Hey, twenty pounds in my book is not bad at all. Maybe you desire to start exercising three days each week, and, in the midst of striving, you begin exercising two days each week. Again, something is better than nothing; two is better than one and one is better than none. Maybe you plan to pray for half an hour each day; although, you don’t quite make it. Something is better than nothing, and at least you are praying for fifteen minutes each day.

The point is we must always strive to better ourselves and move in the right direction, and to do so we must implement discipline; this includes financial discipline.

The Apostle Paul, who I think was one of the most disciplined men ever, put it like this:

But I discipline my body and bring it into subjection, lest, when I have preached to others, I myself should become disqualified.

I Corinthians 9:27

Self-control must be applied to money, the earning, managing, and investing thereof. Remember: money is neutral. How money is used is inevitable. It all begins with the issues of the heart. If you have a limited amount of money, your money must be specifically channeled to the right places. People who have more money have more room to spare. Others have very little wiggle room; therefore, discipline is essential to succeed and move to a higher level. The previous chapter on constructing a plan or budget is great; although, if we never fulfill the plan, the plan can painfully become one more area in life in which we have failed.

May we jump ahead for a minute? I know the thought many of you are entertaining: "I can't wait until I have so much money that I won't have to be so concerned with every penny."

I know where you are going with that thought, and I'm sorry to burst your bubble with the following truth: more money simply brings more responsibility.

"...For everyone to whom much is given, from him much will be required; and to whom much has been committed, of him they will ask the more."

Luke 12:48

Our goal should not be to exercise self-control until we no longer need self-control. Rather, our goal should be to learn and implement self-control, thus maintaining self-control for the rest of our lives. If God blesses you with much, He intends for you to bless others as you glorify Him.

This brings us to the million-dollar question: how do you get self-control? How do you become disciplined? Many of us desire self-control. If self-control, in fact, was so easy to obtain, we would all be much more self-controlled people, right?

Why is it that some people have more self-control than others? Some people are driven to work twelve hours each day. Others can hardly pull themselves from the couch. Some people eat healthy food all-day-every-day. Others would rather die than eat vegetables and drink water. Some people compete in triathlons. Others hate to exert energy while looking for the remote.

The truth is different people are motivated by different factors. Some people were raised in homes of discipline; therefore, discipline is a consistent part of their lives. Others face serious situations each day, whether financial or career-related, and there is no option but to work at full-speed all the time. Others are not as motivated for themselves as much as they are motivated for other people; a parent, child, spouse, and etc. Others have survived life-threatening experiences, and they are determined to live life to the fullest for the remainder of their days.

Here are my two cents regarding discipline, and, please know, this is coming from a person who must work at being disciplined; I like to have a good time, and discipline does not always come naturally to me. Whatever form of motivation is driving you: make sure it is a positive form of motivation. Let me clarify. I believe in being driven by factors such as love and purpose. I do not believe in being driven by factors such as fear and pride. When I use the word *fear*, I am not referencing the fear of losing your job or home if you do not show for work. I do not consider that operating in *fear* as much as I consider that *responsibility*. Rather, I think of fear as rejection over acceptance; approval addiction. I have found that when people are driven by factors such as fear, pride, revenge, or even hatred, these motives eventually unravel and there is an unhealthy episode to follow.

Pursue peace with all people, and holiness, without which no one will see the Lord: looking carefully lest anyone fall short of the grace of God; lest any root of bitterness springing up cause trouble, and by this many become defiled.

Hebrews 12:14, 15

Case in point: there have been times in my life when someone has made me look badly. Immediately, my instinctive reflex is to make them look badly. Furthermore, while I am at home thinking on my next encounter with that person, my mind searches for a way to even the score. In other words, I set out with a premeditated plot on how to tear them down, which is not godly, which is not righteous. Can I share with you that this never goes well; it always unravels. Why does it unravel? Because I was motivated with either fear or pride and not motivated with love.

A soft answer turns away wrath,

But a harsh word stirs up anger.

Proverbs 15:1

There is no fear in love; but perfect love casts out fear, because fear involves torment. But he who fears has not been made perfect in love.

1 John 4:18

Self-control should be based on healthy motivation, and--here is the second and my favorite part--self-control is something we can ask of God. I love it! Even when it comes to the most difficult areas of life, we can ask our Heavenly Father for help.

"So I say to you, ask, and it will be given to you; seek, and you will find; knock, and it will be opened to you. For everyone who asks receives, and he who seeks finds, and to him who knocks it will be opened.

Luke 11:9, 10

Therefore rejoice, you fellow strugglers with discipline; there is help to be found.

We previously read that self-control is listed with the fruit of the Spirit in the fifth chapter of Galatians. Thus, we must pray and ask God to help us with self-control. We must admit that we have a weakness, and we are in need of His help. When we humble ourselves and admit the need for a savior in our situation, God is an ever-present help in time of trouble.

God is our refuge and strength,

A very present help in trouble.

Psalm 46:1

Remember:

"...God resists the proud,

But gives grace to the humble."

James 4:6

Ask God to grant you self-control to stay within the confines of the financial plan you have set. Believe me: it will take self-control to succeed at your plan. I know this is difficult to digest, but you will tell yourself *no* many times to stay within your budget. Let me keep sharing tough news with you while we are on a roll: you will tell yourself *no* more times than *yes* to stay within your budget. Think of it this way: if you have tried to set a financial plan many times, and if you have failed many times, it is time to try something new. Ask God to help you. Ask Him to improve your self-control.

Here is some good news to offset the tough news: if God can create the universe, create the human race, heal the sick, raise the dead, turn water into wine, and part the Red Sea, is it not fair to state that He can help us with self-control? Furthermore, if God grants you brand new, supernatural self-control in one swoop, and if you are instantly able to accomplish any task, wonderful! Good for you! Go conquer the world. However, regarding the rest of us, we must understand that, even after asking God to help us, this process will still take effort on our parts.

Evaluate the manner in which you spend money and ask God which habits you must let go. Once you have discerned these habits, ask God to help you let go of these habits. I am not conveying it will be easy, but I am conveying it can be done. Isn't that the news we all want to hear? It can be done.

Let me shift the subject of this chapter to me. As I was struggling to get my book career going, there were many times when my wife and I opted to eat at home. It became very difficult when church would conclude to watch everyone head to all the nearby restaurants. As a matter of fact, I dealt with some hard feelings because I watched people go to restaurants with great frequency when I knew for a fact that my wife and I were in better financial shape than they were. Nevertheless, rather than growing jealous or bitter, my wife and I stuck to the plan we knew God had helped us formulate. Furthermore, even though it may have been tough not going out to eat as often as we would have desired, we did not die from eating at home.

Since I referenced my wife, this is a good opportunity to share another component of successful self-control: accountability. You may have never considered this before, but accountability is a gift from God. Having a person to whom you are accountable--causing you to climb higher--is a blessing and not a curse. One way to begin climbing the mountain of self-control is to get a boost from someone else.

First and foremost, accountability is a precept found in the Word of God.

Confess your trespasses to one another, and pray for one another, that you may be healed. The effective, fervent prayer of a righteous man avails much.

James 5:16

Some biblical translations use the word *trespasses*, others use the words *faults* or *sins*. The point is when we have a weakness in life, such as self-control, it is golden to find a person in whom we can confide for the purpose of growth and improvement.

Let me give you an example of how being accountable to someone can help your endeavor to be more financially self-controlled. Maybe you have difficulty saving money. If you have a trustworthy confidant, a faithful accountability partner, you can give your savings to them and have them hold it for you. You can take it a step farther and give them a schedule in which you will give them more savings each month. You can take it a step farther and give them permission to ask an explanation of you when you ask for your savings back.

Maybe you are too impulsive when it comes to using debit/credit cards. Hand your card to your accountability partner for safe keeping from others and from you. You might be thinking, "But what it if I see something I immediately need, and I do not have my card with me?" Exactly! We need to begin differentiating between luxury and necessity. We need to throttle down our impulsive financial decisions. Many times in life if something is important today it will be important tomorrow, and we can get it then if necessary.

My wife and I hold one another accountable regarding our spending. Out of courtesy, we let one another know when one of us spends money. We do this not out of bondage or to burden one another; rather, it helps us justify when to say *yes* to a purchase or when to say *no*. When you have an accountability partner, it makes you stop and think twice before you make a purchase. It makes you think, "How will I explain the necessity of this purchase to them? Therefore, is this purchase necessary?"

Also concerning my wife, it came to my cognizance one day that I was very good at constructing our financial plan and executing a high percentage of the plan. However, I finally realized that I was not skilled at executing every facet of the plan. I had to admit that I had a weakness with saving money.

My personality typically recognizes the immediate need. There is always a need in my eyes. The house always needs work. The car always needs minor service or repair. Again, there is always an immediate need everywhere I look. However, one of the greatest needs we will all face is the need for emergency savings. I readily admit: my wife is better at saving money than I am. Therefore, I oversee most of the budget, but she is in charge of our savings, and I readily admit that she does a much better job than I ever could.

I encourage you to ask God to help you with self-control. Furthermore, I encourage you to ask God to lay on your heart an accountability partner to help you stay on track. Even the best, most elaborate financial plan or budget in the world is powerless in the hands of a weak person. All it becomes in the end is another task we failed to complete. Self-control gives you the power to complete the task in front of you.

I would like to stop and pray for self-control for you and for me because I need it as much as anyone.

Father, in the name of Jesus, we come to You. You are the best, and we want to be pleasing to You. Help us with self-control. Grant us more self-control. We admit we have a weakness in this area, and we need Your help. We have tried it on our own, and now we desire to try it Your way and with Your help. Father, even lay someone on our hearts and minds in whom we can confide and to whom we can be accountable. Even prepare their hearts before we approach them and let the collaboration come together and be of You, bringing You glory and blessing others along the way. We thank You by faith, knowing that You will help us, and that we will get better. It is wonderful serving You. We ask all of this in the name of Jesus. Amen.

Chapter Twenty-nine

The Secrets and Mysteries of the Kingdom of God

And the disciples came and said to Him, "Why do You speak to them in parables?" He (Jesus) answered and said to them, "Because it has been given to you to know the mysteries of the kingdom of heaven, but to them it has not been given."

Matthew 13:10, 11

It pays to know God. I do not state this in a materialistic sense, as in God pays off as would a slot machine. No, I mean regarding every area of life: it is of great benefit to know God.

It is of great benefit to know God if you need salvation, healing, relational restoration, financial restoration, and etc. It is of great benefit to know God because God has the inside track regarding all things spiritual and physical. Who could offer better advice regarding all things than the Creator of all things? Not only has God created all things, He has created the system for success. God, in other words, knows how the system works. This applies to financial matters. Remember, it would be incorrect and foolish for us to exclude God from any area of our lives; if so, we need an alignment adjustment.

"And you shall remember the Lord your God, for it is He who gives you power to get wealth, that He may establish His covenant which He swore to your fathers, as it is this day."

Deuteronomy 8:18

By the way, which is better: wealth or the power to get wealth? Obviously, the power to get wealth lasts in perpetuity. God wants to educate His children in the power to get wealth and prosper—and why—to glorify Him and bless others.

When we obtain or attempt to obtain wealth in our own wisdom and strength, there will be failure. Even those who seem to have everything and who have obtained wealth through deceit, lying, and backstabbing have strings attached to their wealth. These strings will undoubtedly pull one day, and both their wealth and tactics will be exposed. It is God who gives us power to get wealth by righteousness. This type of wealth is not a precarious, flimsy wealth. Rather, this wealth is built on a sure foundation and will withstand the storms and persecutions of life.

The power to get wealth by righteousness comes from God. The wisdom to get wealth by righteousness comes from God. The secret to get wealth by righteousness comes from God.

"'Call to Me, and I will answer you, and show you great and mighty things, which you do not know.'"

Jeremiah 33:3

Oh, the depth of the riches both of the wisdom and knowledge of God! How unsearchable are His judgments and His ways past finding out!

"For who has known the mind of the Lord?

Or who has become His counselor?

Or who has first given to Him

And it shall be repaid to him?"

For of Him and through Him and to Him are all things, to whom be glory forever. Amen.

Romans 11:33-36

"No longer do I call you servants, for a servant does not know what his master is doing; but I have called you friends, for all things that I heard from My Father I have made known to you."

John 15:15

It is of great benefit to know God. It is of great benefit to enter the kingdom of salvation through faith in the blood of Jesus. The Word of God teaches us concerning all things, including how to succeed financially. Furthermore, the ways and methods to succeed are at the disposal of God, and they are endless.

- God may open the door for you to apply and work at a certain place, knowing that one day you will be discovered there and relocated to the next place.
- God may open the door for you to go to college and earn beyond a graduate degree.
- God may open the door for you to begin a business.
- God may open the door for you to join a business.
- God may lay on your heart a book or curriculum to write.
- God may lay on your heart a mentor from whom to learn.
- God may lay on your heart the need to volunteer for free to get your foot in the door.
- God may lay on your heart a keen invention to enhance the lives of others.

I wisdom dwell with prudence, and find out knowledge of witty inventions.

Proverbs 8:12 KJV

Who knows what God has in store for you? Actually, we know the answer to that question. God knows what He has in store for you, and His plans for you are wonderful. Is it not time for you to know what God has for you? Is it not worth sitting at His feet and seeking His wisdom for your life? His wisdom for your life is more valuable than any degree of education you could obtain. It is great to seek high school, collegiate, and mastery education;

however, a master's degree is not your source of provision. God is your source of provision. Therefore, if God opens the door for you to pursue a master's degree, do it; that would be wonderful. Just make sure to keep first things first.

I am next going to step on some toes and rattle traditional thinking. We have watched it happen for years: the *have's* and the *have-not's*. We watch as those with money have avenues such as college, social status, and overall networking to a better life. Let me state it for the record: you do not have to be born into a wealthy family to have success in the kingdom of God; you simply have to be born into the kingdom of God.

The power to get wealth, the mysteries of the kingdom of God, and the wisdom for witty inventions are accessible to all those who humble themselves and enter relationship with God. There is no need to fear because you were not born into a wealthy family. Rather, humble yourself and be born by the Spirit into the wealthiest family of all with the wealthiest Father of all.

Yes, others have an easier road on the surface. Yes, your road will take hard work. Yes, you will have to work harder at times than many people. However, your road to wealth is a sure road, a certain road, and a guaranteed road. I cannot account for how life will materialize for others, but I can promise you that life will go well for you if you follow the ways of God. Yes, I promise you. Even better, not only will life go well for you, but eternal life will go very well for you.

Surely goodness and mercy shall follow me

All the days of my life;

And I will dwell in the house of the Lord

Forever.

Psalm 23:6

So, the question is…are you in or out? Are you on board or off the board? Are you with Him or against Him? There is no middle ground to be found in this case. Serving God is an all or nothing proposition.

"So then, because you are lukewarm, and neither cold nor hot, I will vomit you out of My mouth."

Revelation 3:16

The previous verse addresses the nature of God as He looks for those who are fully committed to Him, not even those who are partially committed.

Is your life a mystery to you? Do you question how you will arrive at the next level? Be encouraged: there is unbridled potential to be discovered in your relationship with God. He is ready to reveal the mystery of your life to you.

Chapter Thirty

Was Jesus Poor?

This is a question that should be asked and addressed more often. There are those both inside and outside the church who suggest that children of God should be poor. Many inside the church believe it is correct to be poor to protect ourselves from materialism. Many outside the church believe it is correct for children of God to be poor to keep us from appearing as hypocritical opportunists.

I relish the opportunity to answer both perspectives. I am not an opportunist who changes my principles to suit myself or anyone else for that matter; however, I take the opportunity to prosper financially, which is afforded me by my Heavenly Father.

Beloved, I pray that you may prosper in all things and be in health, just as your soul prospers.

3 John verse 2

Trust in the Lord with all your heart,

And lean not on your own understanding;

In all your ways acknowledge Him,

And He shall direct your paths.

Proverbs 3:5, 6

In all your ways includes the area of my money. My financial motive is not to get for the sake of getting; rather, my motive is to get for the sake of giving more. I am sure there are many people outside the church who strive simply for the sake of getting, so the hypocrisy argument does not stick to me as much as to them.

Regarding those within the kingdom of God who believe children of God should be poor: my answer to them is...check your Bible. Do not check theological, philosophical, religious, or denominational handbooks; instead, check your Bible.

Let them shout for joy and be glad,

Who favor My righteous cause;

And let them say continually,

"Let the Lord be magnified,

Who has pleasure in the prosperity of His servant."

And my tongue shall speak of Your righteousness

And of Your praise all the day long.

Psalm 35:27, 28

As in any given situation, I believe the best example to follow is the life of Jesus. As it pertains to doubts or questions regarding any discussion, who serves as a better model, blueprint, and paradigm than Jesus Christ Himself?

This brings us back to the question...was Jesus poor?

What do we know of Jesus in summation? Jesus has always existed with the Father; They are One. He came to earth from heaven. He was born in humility in a manger normally reserved for animals. He had a modest upbringing from what we can gather, possibly serving as an apprentice to his father before becoming a carpenter Himself (a humble vocation, no doubt). Even so, He could have worked for middle-class and upper-class people alike as a carpenter. Jesus later travelled extensively and ministered, bringing the gospel of salvation and healing to all those who would hear while covering a vast area. Jesus was eventually arrested, tried, sentenced, beaten, and crucified on a cross. He laid down His life, was buried, rose from the dead, and ultimately ascended to the Father in heaven where he is poised to return to earth again.

Again, Jesus at the time of His birth was found in a lowly manger because there was not room for Him and His parents elsewhere. However, gifts were presented to Him at the arrival of the wise men from the east: gold, frankincense, and myrrh (each gift displaying physical and spiritual symbolism).

And when they had come into the house, they saw the young Child with Mary His mother, and fell down and worshipped Him. And when they had opened their treasures, they presented gifts to Him: gold, frankincense, and myrrh.

Matthew 2:11

It was very possible that these gifts served as currency for Joseph to get his family from Bethlehem to Egypt to safely await the death of King Herod. I don't know the likelihood of Joseph having enough savings to make such a spontaneous journey to escape. Therefore, by the presentation of these gifts of monetary value, Jesus and His family had what they needed when they needed it.

Later in His life, Jesus, at the age of twelve, was found in the temple after multiple days of absence from the care of His parents. Found sitting with the teachers while both listening and answering questions, His response to His frantically perplexed parents was very matter of fact.

And He said to them, "Why did you seek Me? Did you not know that I must be about My Father's business?"

Luke 2:49

Obviously, Jesus had to receive benevolent care in the temple to be absent from His parents for three days. Jesus, at the very least, would have received food and lodging during His stay. Therefore, Jesus had what He needed when He needed it.

The Bible is silent regarding Jesus and most of His years of adolescence and early adulthood. We resume learning of His life just before His ministry began. He embarked on a forty-day fast, which concluded in a confrontation with Satan. Please note: the fast on which Jesus embarked was not because of a lack of money; rather, this was a fast of choice and submission. The Bible never indicates that Jesus was denied food because of a lack of money. The Bible simply states:

And when He had fasted forty days and forty nights, afterward He was hungry.

Matthew 4:2

Jesus began His ministry, thus commenced the travelling and the miracles. The miracles included raising the dead, opening eyes and ears, and casting out demons. Also, the miracles included the transformation of water into wine.

And when they ran out of wine, the mother of Jesus said to Him, "They have no wine." Jesus said to them, "Fill the waterpots with water." And they filled them up to the brim.

John 2:3, 7

The transformation of water to wine displayed the ability of Jesus to take that of little monetary value and make it of great monetary worth. Obviously, water is essential to live, but it is also abundant in many places. The manufacturing of wine takes effort, laborers, land, and grapes from a vineyard of produce. Even when taking something of lesser value and making it of greater value, Jesus had what He needed when He needed it.

Another instance of taking little and making much in the hands of Jesus are the famous accounts of Him feeding crowds of thousands.

When it was evening, His disciples came to Him, saying, "This is a deserted place, and the hour is already late. Send the multitudes away, that they may go into the villages and buy themselves food." But Jesus said to them, "They do not need to go away. You give them something to eat." And they said to Him, "We have here only five loaves and two fish." He said, "Bring them here to Me." Then He commanded the multitudes to sit down on the grass. And He took the five loaves and the two fish, and looking up to heaven, He blessed and broke and gave the loaves to the disciples; and the disciples gave to the multitudes. So they all ate

and were filled, and they took up twelve baskets full of the fragments that remained. Now those who had eaten were about five thousand men, besides women and children.

Matthew 14:15-21

What a miracle! Jesus took little, gave honor to the Father while blessing what little He had, and He and the Father transformed little into much. The numbers in the crowd were staggering that day: five thousand men plus women and children. Let us guess there were twenty-thousand people present that day just to be conservative. Twenty-thousand were fed from what began as five loaves of bread and two fish, and this is the same God of multiplication we serve (notice in this account how God was glorified and others were blessed).

There is another account of Jesus feeding multitudes while using very little, and it is clear, once we take the time to evaluate the life of Jesus as a whole: Jesus was a man who financially had what He needed when He needed it. Furthermore, the fact that Jesus was blessed was a blessing to others.

One of my favorite stories in the Bible pertaining to financial provision in the life of Jesus is found in the following verse. Notice the response from Jesus when confronted with premise of paying taxes.

"Nevertheless, lest we offend them, go to the sea, cast in a hook, and take the fish that comes up first. And when you have opened its mouth, you will find a piece of money; take that and give it to them for Me and you."

Matthew 17:27

This account summarizes the life of Jesus from a financial perspective in my opinion: Jesus had what He needed when He needed it. Whether paying taxes, feeding twenty-thousand people, or transforming something of little monetary value into something of much monetary value, Jesus had what He needed when He needed it. Yes, Jesus was a man of sorrow and suffering as foretold by the Old Testament. However, it is important to understand that Jesus embraced this lifestyle of suffering by His own freewill. He often denied Himself food. He often denied Himself extravagant accommodations. People often use the following verse to try to support their belief that Jesus was poor.

Then a certain scribe came and said to Him, "Teacher, I will follow You wherever You go." And Jesus said to Him, "Foxes have holes and birds of the air have nests, but the Son of Man has nowhere to lay His head."

Matthew 8:19, 20

It is important to understand that Jesus was not referencing a state of poverty when expressing that He had nowhere to lay his head. Rather, Jesus was expressing that--by following Him--the scribe must be willing to forsake all.

Jesus lived and moved with purpose. It was not that His life was destitute because of poverty or lack; rather, He often did not burden Himself with objects and possessions that would deter His mission on earth. It would not make much since for an extensively travelling minister to have numerous possessions weighing Him down while on the road. Again, when we study the scriptures, we find that Jesus had what He needed when He needed it.

As a matter of fact, Jesus had others who followed Him; individuals who ministered to Him and His disciples as they travelled and ministered to people. Jesus also travelled in the company of a designated treasurer who we know to be Judas Iscariot. Obviously, there would only be need for a treasurer if there were treasures (money) to oversee. It is obvious that it would take money to accommodate such a group as they ministered from town to town and city to city.

Moreover, it is important to note the opposite end of the spectrum pertaining to money and the life of Jesus. Jesus was not money-hungry. Jesus was not materialistic. Jesus did not abuse His power. Finally, Jesus did not see the ministry of God as means to profiteer and line His pockets. A perfect example was the anger Jesus displayed toward the money changers and those who bought and sold in the temple.

And He said to them, "It is written, 'My house shall be called a house of prayer,' but you have made it a 'den of thieves.'"

Matthew 21:13

The scriptures give record of Jesus...

- Having what He needed when He needed it
- Receiving the benefits from wealthy financiers such as the wise men who brought gifts to Him as a child and the wealthy Joseph of Arimathea who laid the body of Jesus to rest in his personal tomb (Jesus had everything He needed from birth to death and from beginning to end)
- Bringing His tithes and offerings to the temple
- Disdaining those who attempted to profiteer in the temple
- Paying taxes
- Blessing and giving to others through preaching, teaching, time, miracles, and food
- Refusing to worship Satan in exchange for all the riches of the kingdoms of the world

As we summarize the life of Jesus regarding money, it is no surprise that Jesus is the shining financial example for our lives. He was a man on earth who understood the importance and significance of money; yet, He was not materialistic. It is fair to state that Jesus was a good student and practitioner of business. He worked hard, and He knew success in life and business came at a price.

"For which of you, intending to build a tower, does not sit down first and count the cost, whether he has enough to finish it—lest, after he has laid the foundation, and is not able to finish, all who see it begin to mock him, saying, 'This man began to build and was not able to finish?'"

Luke 14:28-30

Jesus was a man who taught on the concept of money yet always pointed to those things of the most value and worth. Jesus knew that money had both physical and spiritual value. I believe, more than anything, Jesus used the importance of money to explain what is most important. If someone cannot recognize and take care of what is important (money), how can he or she recognize and take care of what is most important (eternal life).

"He who is faithful in what is least is faithful also in much; and he who is unjust in what is least is unjust also in much. Therefore if you have not been faithful in unrighteous mammon, who will commit to your trust the true riches? And if you have not been faithful in what is another man's, who will give you what is your own?"

Luke 16:10-12

"For what profit is it to a man if he gains the whole world, and loses his own soul? Or what will a man give in exchange for his soul?"

Matthew 16:26

As we turn to the scriptures, and not opinions, conjecture, or philosophy, we find that Jesus was a man who trusted God for everything He would ever need. Should not we live in the same manner?

Was Jesus poor? No: the word *poor* means to be in lack. Jesus was never in lack. Jesus was a man who financially had what He needed when He needed it. Why would it be wrong for us to aspire to live in the same way?

Chapter Thirty-one

A Lesson in Contentment: Ask Solomon: There Is More to Life than Money

Is this statement true? Is there more to life than money? Who should we ask? Why not ask he who had more money than anyone in the world?

The account goes that King Solomon asked God for wisdom rather than asking for anything else, and God responded in the following way.

"Behold, I have done according to your words; see, I have given you a wise and understanding heart, so that there has not been anyone like you before you, nor shall any like you arise after you. And I have also given you what you have not asked: both riches and honor, so that there shall not be anyone like you among the kings all your days."

1 Kings 3:12, 13

The current-day value of the wealth of Solomon is astronomical. Undoubtedly, all that Solomon ever needed financially he had. Many times we fantasize what it would be like to have such wealth. We often associate wealth with freedom from problems and trials. What we fail to realize is that some problems subside at the sight of wealth while other problems appear because of wealth. I am not referencing wealth as a negative attribute in life; rather, I am expressing the truth regarding wealth, that wealth it is not our savior, and that wealth does not cure all the cares of life. The words of Solomon testify as such.

Riches do not profit in the day of wrath,

But righteousness delivers from death.

Proverbs 11:4

He who trusts in his riches will fall,

But the righteous will flourish like foliage.

Proverbs 11:28

Better is a little with the fear of the Lord,

Than great treasure with trouble.

Proverbs 15:16

Better is little with righteousness,

Than vast revenues without justice.

Proverbs 16:8

Better is the poor who walks in his integrity

Than one who is perverse in his lips, and is a fool.

Proverbs 19:1

"Vanity of vanities," says the Preacher;

"Vanity of vanities, all is vanity."

What profit has a man from all his labor

In which he toils under the sun?

All things are full of labor;

Man cannot express it.

The eye is not satisfied with seeing,

Nor the ear filled with hearing."

Ecclesiastes 1:2, 3, 8

I made my works great, I built myself houses, and planted myself vineyards. I made myself gardens and orchards, and I planted all kinds of fruit trees in them. I made myself water pools from which to water the growing trees of the grove. I acquired male and female servants, and had servants born in my house. Yes, I had greater possessions of herds and flocks than all who were in Jerusalem before me. I also gathered for myself silver and gold and the special treasures of kings and of the provinces. I acquired male and female singers, the delights of the sons of men, and musical instruments of all kinds. So I became great and excelled more than all who were before me in Jerusalem. Also my wisdom remained with me.

Whatever my eyes desired I did not keep from them.

I did not withhold my heart from any pleasure,

For my heart rejoiced in all my labor;

And this was my reward from all my labor.

Then I looked on all the works that my hands had done

And on the labor in which I had toiled;

And indeed all was vanity and grasping for the wind.

There was no profit under the sun.

Ecclesiastes 2:4-11

Better a poor and wise youth

Than an old and foolish king who will be admonished no more.

Ecclesiastes 4:13

The sleep of a laboring man is sweet,

Whether he eats little or much;

But the abundance of the rich will not permit him to sleep.

Ecclesiastes 5:12

All the labor of man is for his mouth,

And yet the soul is not satisfied.

Ecclesiastes 6:7

There is more to life than money; ask a man who had it all.

It is essential to be driven in life for the right reasons and with the right motives. It is a dangerous place to be when you strive and strive and strive, and then you finally arrive, only to find that what you have found is not what you want.

Wealthy people are not that different from destitute people. Wealthy people get depressed. Wealthy people have marital problems and get divorced. Wealthy people are human, and they deal with sickness and death like everyone else. Furthermore, it is worthless to strive for wealth the wrong way, sacrificing morals, family, and friends to gain what you always thought you desired. When a person invests years to get to that point, only to find that satisfaction is not to be found, the sorrow is overwhelming.

There is something to be said for living a simple life. I am not expressing that you should quit striving and reaching for your financial goals. No, I am expressing that if you have a simple life…enjoy it. Bigger homes mean more square-footage to clean and maintain. Second homes mean more to oversee. More cars mean more insurance. Boats mean more consumption of time. I keep coming back to the same verse:

"…For everyone to whom much is given, from him much will be required; and to whom much has been committed, of him they will ask the more."

Luke 12:48

As I wrote earlier, it is a blessing to learn from your mistakes; however, it is an even greater blessing to learn from the mistakes of others before you make the same mistakes. Take it from Solomon: money by itself is meaningless. Furthermore, life is meaningless apart from the One who gives meaning to life.

My final comments of this chapter are these: our little girl is a planner. She cracks us up. She would plan our entire week with activities if we would let her. One of her mandates from planning is that Monday night is *family board game night*!

One night we picked an old-school game: the board game Life. You may or may not have played this game. We had a great time because in the game of Life you choose whether to attend college or immediately start a career, you earn a salary, you get married along the way, you add children along the way, and life hands you good times and bad. Therefore, we lived an approximately eighty-year lifespan in about an hour.

Well, the game ended, and we were left to count what we had accumulated. We counted our assets and our cash, and we compared to see who had the most. I did not tell my wife and kids this because we had a great time together, and I didn't want to be a wet blanket. Even so, after having a great time at the game of Life, honestly, the following thought went through my head when it was all over: what's the point? What's the point of who has the most money? What's the point of all the assets when the game is finished? Obviously, I believe in leaving a financial legacy for my children. I am simply referencing the material objects we acquire in life. What's the point?

Please know: what comes after life is what's most important. There is *more* to life than just money, so make sure you find what the *more* is before your life ends.

Chapter Thirty-two

An Encouraging Word to the Young

Start now! Start applying the principles of the Bible to your money now. The earlier you start the earlier you will see blessings come to pass. Also, the earlier you begin trusting God and His ways the easier it will be to trust Him when you are older. Our children are very young while I am writing this book, and I cannot wait to teach them the biblical principles of money, tithing, and sowing and reaping.

Then the little children were brought to Him that He might put His hands on them and pray, but the disciples rebuked them. But Jesus said, "Let the little children come to Me, and do not forbid them; for of such is the kingdom of heaven."

Matthew 19:13, 14

Let no one despise your youth, but be an example to the believers in word, in conduct, in love, in spirit, in faith, in purity.

1 Timothy 4:12

As I referenced earlier, I am excited to teach my children the principle of giving and receiving. We have already given them money to give while in church, yet I look forward to the day when they set their hands to work and earn their first dollar. My wife and I have already begun sitting and sharing with them that everything we have is given by God. We have explained to them that apart from God there is nothing. God provides one-hundred percent of all that we have, yet He asks for a mere ten percent with which to begin.

I encourage the youth reading this book: start now. Start applying biblical principles to your money now. There will come a day when you will need a job, a car, money for college and books, and etc. How wonderful if you would start sowing seed now. Sometimes the harvest takes a while to grow and mature. There is no better time than now to begin sowing seed for your future.

Children and youth, start now. Start applying biblical principles to your money now. Give and ask God to meet the financial needs before you. Even if a car, college, and a place to live seem far in the distance, these seasons in life will be here before you know it. Start sowing today in the rich soil of the kingdom of God, and He will bless you in your future day of need.

Chapter Thirty-three

An Encouraging Word to the...Older

I do not use the word *older* with disrespect. The truth is we all grow older and there is no way to keep this from happening. I graduated from my teens to my twenties to my thirties seemingly overnight. Growing older is part of life. We might as well embrace this fact and know that God still desires to do great things in our lives. Furthermore, knowing God becomes sweeter with each passing year.

One generation shall praise Your works to another,

And shall declare Your mighty acts.

Psalm 145:4

Seasons arrive, and we must shift our focus. When I became a husband, my focus shifted to my wife. When we became parents, our focus shifted to our children.

Whether you have children or not, there comes a time when your focus must shift from meeting your needs to meeting the needs of the next generation. My pastor shared a sobering thought with our church recently. He informed us that those in the congregation of forty years and older need to make caring for the next generation their primary concern.

I believe it is only right to desire better for our children than we had for ourselves. I am not discarding the value of hard work while handing my children everything; not at all. I will certainly share with my children the truth: they will have to work hard for the rest of their lives to be successful. Rather, I desire is for my children to not start from the beginning. I desire for them to build on what I have accomplished and learned, just as I built on what my parents accomplished and learned. Please understand, I am different from my parents, and my children are different from me. I do not desire for my children to be like me in personality or individuality. I simply desire for them to have everything they need to succeed. My parents worked very hard to get us to a certain financial checkpoint. I have taken the baton from there, and, by the grace of God, I will take my family to a new financial checkpoint, and I hope my children will do the same for their children.

Therefore, if I desire for this to happen, if I desire for my children to succeed beyond my success, at some point I must lay my selfish concerns aside and put the next generation ahead of me. It will require me sitting with my children and teaching them. It will require me investing time while putting aside some of the work I need to complete, knowing that unless I train the next generation the feats I have accomplished will be erased, and my children will start from scratch due to a lack of wisdom and knowledge.

"For in this the saying is true: 'One sows and another reaps.' I sent you to reap that for which you have not labored; others have labored, and you have entered into their labors."

John 4:37, 38

We all learn from someone while on this earth. This truth is inevitable. Even if we have learned what not to do based on the mistakes of others, we have still learned from them. The next generation will learn from us one way or another. They will either learn to do what we teach them or what we don't teach them.

I ask you to think back on your life. Someone was there to help you along the way, weren't they? Maybe it was a parent, a brother or sister, an uncle or aunt, a friend of the family, a neighbor, a teacher, a pastor, or someone in your church. If you think hard enough, someone helped you along the way to get where you are today. Whether they let you stay rent-free in their home, helped you get that first beat-up car, or gave you an interest-free loan to buy books for college, someone helped you along the way. Even if you had a difficult life on reflection, God still sent someone to help you along the way to get you to this point. If nothing else, God sent someone to get you to this point so someday you would help someone else.

If we think hard enough, God sent a financier somewhere along the line to help in our time of need. I encourage all of us, while we are alive and breathing, while we are alive and have the power to do so, let us be a financier for someone else.

Maybe it is letting your children live at home until they can one day move out debt free? I am not endorsing enabling or freeloading; maybe work out a reasonable rent-for-savings arrangement. Why just throw them out on the street to fend for their own? Wouldn't this be better than them beginning life under a mountain of debt at the age of eighteen? Maybe it is selling your car for next to nothing to a nephew or niece who is trying to work and go to school at the same time? Maybe it is finding a college kid in your church and offering to buy their books for the upcoming semester? Maybe it is something as small as sending a child to summer church camp or Vacation Bible School? Maybe it is something as big as leaving an inheritance to an individual or a ministry?

The list of what you can do is endless. I just encourage you, since God sent a financier to you during your time of need, be a financier to someone else. Let us leave a legacy of love in the name of Jesus Christ.

Chapter Thirty-four

A Pic of What God Is Doing

Draw near to God and He will draw near to you....

James 4:8

This verse has been great help to me through the years; although, recently I have come to a fuller understanding of these words. I always thought of this verse in simple terms, meaning if I draw near to God in prayer, He will draw near to me, and this is correct to a large degree. God is faithful, and if I pray in faith, He will honor my faith and meet me where I am.

I have come to understand that not only can I draw near God in prayer, but I can draw near God by drawing near to the ways of God. That is, I draw near God when I am obedient to His way of living. Again, who knows how to live better than the One with the blueprint for living? The Bible is the blueprint for living...and living successfully. The Bible is the Word of God. The Bible teaches us the ways of God. Therefore, I can successfully draw near to God by drawing near to the ways of God.

I am reminded of the words of Jesus:

For this is the love of God, that we keep His commandments. And His commandments are not burdensome.

1 John 5:3

If you need salvation, draw near to the ways of God and learn of salvation. If you need healing, draw near to the ways of God and learn of healing. If you need relational restoration, draw near to the ways of God and learn of relational restoration. If you need wisdom, draw near to the ways of God and learn of wisdom. Furthermore, if you need financial prosperity, draw near to the ways of God and learn of financial prosperity.

You will, in fact, draw near to God as you draw near to the ways of God. What are the ways of God regarding biblical financial prosperity? The ways of God are to bring the tithe. The ways of God are to give offerings above the tithe; sow seed. The ways of God are to bless others in need. The ways of God are to work hard and ask the blessing of the Lord on your work. The ways of God are to know the state of your resources. The ways of God are to pay any bills and debt that you owe. The ways of God are to act wisely and store savings. The ways of God are to show self-restraint from impulsivity when managing money. The ways of God are to not seek riches hastily, thus exercising diligence and patience while not gambling with your money.

When you draw near to the ways of God, meaning when you trust that the ways of God are best for you and your money, you are drawing near to God.

"For My thoughts are not your thoughts,

Nor are your ways My ways," says the Lord.

"For as the heavens are higher than the earth,

So are My ways higher than your ways,

And My thoughts than your thoughts."

Isaiah 55:8, 9

Blessed are the undefiled in the way,

Who walk in the law of the Lord!

Blessed are those who keep His testimonies,

Who seek Him with the whole heart!

They also do no iniquity;

They walk in His ways.

Psalm 119:1-3

We have studied the ways of God in this book, referencing the instructions of the Bible at every turn. We have, by doing so, drawn near to God by drawing near to the ways of God. This is what we have done and what we will continue to do. Now, the questions is, what will God do?

Draw near to God and He will draw near to you….

James 4:8

God will draw near to us. Not only will He draw near to us when we pray, but He will draw near to us in the same areas in which we draw to Him.

If you draw near to the ways of God regarding salvation, God will draw near with salvation. If you draw near to the ways of God regarding healing, God will draw near with healing. If you draw near to the ways of God regarding relational restoration, God will draw near with relational restoration. If you draw near to the ways of God regarding wisdom, God will draw near with wisdom. Therefore, if you draw near to the ways of God regarding financial prosperity, yes, God will draw near with financial prosperity.

Here is a pic of what God is doing in the area of your money. As you draw near to the ways of God by bringing your tithe, giving offerings, blessing those in need, working hard, knowing the state of your resources, paying any bills and debt that you owe, acting wisely and storing savings, showing self-restraint from impulsivity when managing money, and exercising diligence while not seeking riches hastily, He will draw near to you in ways you cannot imagine. As you draw near to God through the ways of God, God is opening doors, God is granting favor, God is moving people in and moving people out, and God is laying your name on the hearts of others who have much influence.

God, in short, is doing the impossible. God is making things happen that are impossible for you to make happen. God is making things happen that are beyond your ability to make happen. God is even making things happen that are beyond your creativity to imagine. How can God do these things? Simple, He is God.

But Jesus looked at them and said to them, "With men this is impossible, but with God all things are possible."

Matthew 19:26

I know what some of you are thinking. You are recalling the episode in which you prayed and trusted God to perform the impossible, and it never happened. Well, get in line behind me. I have experienced that episode more times than I can count. However, if you look deeply enough and remember well enough, you may remember that the situation did not seem to change, but God changed you. God changed you by bringing His peace into the room, by bringing His joy into the room, by bringing His contentment into the room, by bringing Himself into the room.

You did draw near to God, and He did draw near to you. You performed the possible: you trusted God. God performed the impossible: He changed your heart and helped you endure the situation.

Here is some more good news before this chapter draws to a close. When you do this, when you draw near to God by drawing near to the ways of God, the One working on the other end of your situation is not an ordinary man. Rather, this is the God of the universe working on your situation. Therefore, the probability is very high that He will more than meet you halfway. I have found that when I draw near to the ways of God on my part, the end result always appears more quickly than I anticipated. The home loan, in other words, gets paid off more quickly than in thirty years. The car gets paid off more quickly than in five years. The overwhelming credit card debt gets paid off more quickly than I ever dreamed.

Here is a pic of what God is doing: He is doing more than you can ask or think.

Now to Him who is able to do exceedingly abundantly above all that we ask or think, according to the power that works in us, to Him be glory in the church by Christ Jesus to all generations, forever and ever. Amen.

Ephesians 3:20

If you want results, do it your way. However, if you want the highest results, do it God's way because God's ways are higher than your ways.

Chapter Thirty-five

Debt: What Does God Think?

I hope I have earned your trust as you have read this book. More specifically, I hope I have earned your trust in the sense that I desire the best for you. Not only do I desire the best for you, but, more importantly, God desires the best for you. Therefore, I feel I can give you tough news, and you won't instantaneously flee from the following challenge.

Debt is a heavy word, is it not? *Debt* is a word that shivers the spine. Debt is imposing. Debt is formidable. Debt is overwhelming. Debt is a thought that people try to mentally block, yet debt remains beneath the surface, and if not given ample attention, the tide of debt rises high.

I believe a large majority of us have experienced a brush with debt. Some of us have not only experienced a brush with debt, but we have been dyed with the brush of debt. Even the word *debt* is too similar to the word *death* for my taste, which near death is how you feel when immersed in debt.

The thought of debt, on a serious note, can be discouraging, disheartening, and depressing. The mental and emotional weight of debt has led to physical health problems, divorce, suicide, and--I am sure--homicide.

There are a variety of reasons why people fall in debt. The obvious inclination is poor spending habits or overall mismanagement of money. Some, however, have fallen in debt with the best intentions. Some fall in debt when they endure the sky-high financial expense of caring for an ill member of the family. Some innocently fall in debt because of the actions of others. They themselves did nothing to conjure debt, yet here they are.

Some of you, on another serious note, are on the verge of tears as you read the words of this chapter. Some of you literally experience manifestations of anxiety. Your heart-rate increases or your blood pressure rises anytime the subject is broached. Debt is a serious, solemn situation. Some of you feel as if you are literally facing a life or death situation because of mounting financial debt.

I am not attempting to add to your problems by stating the obvious. I am, on the other hand, attempting to bring us to the point where we admit there is a problem. Some of you do not need my help in doing so; you already know there is a problem. Others, however, need to take the first step and admit that you need help beyond your own power. You have tried handling debt your way. Now is the time to handle debt in a different way. Here is some good news. There is a different way. There is a right way. Yes, when it comes to handling debt, be encouraged: God has a way. Amen!

I will be forthright with you in this chapter, but I will be forthright in both directions. What I mean is this: yes, I will share with you the tough news, but I will also share with you the good news because there is good news to be shared regarding financial debt.

Let's go ahead and start there: the good news. The good news is that regardless of how much you are in debt, regardless of the threatening letters you are receiving in the mail, and regardless of the calls you are receiving on your phone, your situation is not impossible. Your situation is not impossible, that is, as long as someone is in your life that can perform the impossible.

Is anything too hard for the Lord?

Genesis 18:14

So shall My word be that goes forth from My mouth;

It shall not return to Me void,

But it shall accomplish what I please,

And it shall prosper in the thing for which I sent it.

Isaiah 55:11

Then the Lord said to me, "You have seen well, for I am ready to perform My word."

Jeremiah 1:12

"For with God nothing will be impossible."

Luke 1:37

"If you ask anything in My name, I will do it."

John 14:14

I understand that the financial debt confronting you is enormous. I understand that there is no logical hope in sight. I understand that you are at the end of your physical, mental, and emotional rope. Nevertheless, the financial debt facing you pales in comparison to the unpardonable debt of sin that once faced all mankind. Sin towered over mankind until the Son of God appeared in the flesh. When all hope for mankind was lost, God sent Jesus, and when God sent Jesus God sent a savior, that whoever would call on the name of the Lord would be saved.

Yes, your looming financial debt may bring great fear with it, but your financial debt is no match in totality for the weight of sin that Jesus bore on the cross. Jesus took sin, shame, and even death, and He carried it all and defeated all enemies; both physical and spiritual. Therefore remember: though your financial debt might seem overwhelming, there is no amount of money that could have appeased the debt of sin. If you have accepted the payment for your sinful debt by casting your faith on the blood of Jesus, rejoice: if He can pay that debt, He can pay this debt.

He who did not spare His own Son, but delivered Him up for us all, how shall He not with Him also freely give us all things?

Romans 8:32

If you have never accepted the payment for your sinful debt by casting your faith on the blood of Jesus, this is the best opportunity you will ever have to do so.

Moving from spiritual to financial debt, as I stated earlier, there are many factors that can lead to debt. Personally, I am not going to cast judgment on you if you are in financial debt. How can I begin to analyze your situation apart from knowing the facts? Rather than waste time judging and looking to the past, let us look forward and strive toward the financial freedom we desire.

As is always the case, we look to the Word of God to receive the instructions of God regarding every area of life. Here are some biblical scriptures regarding financial debt:

My son, if you become surety (a pledge) for your friend,

If you have shaken hands in pledge for a stranger,

You are snared by the words of your mouth;

You are taken by the words of your mouth.

Proverbs 6:1, 2

The rich rules over the poor,

And the borrower is servant to the lender.

Proverbs 22:7

Better not to vow than to vow and not pay.

Ecclesiastes 5:5

Owe no one anything except to love one another, for he who loves another has fulfilled the law.

Romans 13:8

Here is the truth regarding debt in the eyes of God: when you agree to debt, when you enter a financial agreement by stating that you owe money, it is your responsibility to pay that debt. God views your debt as your obligation. If you make an agreement with someone, if you sign a contract, if you shake a hand, or if you even speak the words from your mouth, God ratifies the agreement and your obligation to pay. Please do not make the foolish mistake of entering an agreement while thinking that God will relieve you of your debt once you repent in the morning. God will indeed forgive you; He is faithful and just to forgive. However, regarding the agreement you made with another individual or party, God sees the agreement as binding. He views the debt as your responsibility to pay.

I realize there are different types of debt. There is low-interest debt. There is no-interest debt. There is a certain number of months same as cash. There are agreements and loans between friends. Factor in the different reasons why people get in debt and, again, I am not going to judge anyone without knowing all the details. If a situation is out of your control, and if you must travel across the country to care for a loved one, and if you must borrow cash from a family member or friend to do so, I will not sit here and condemn you. However, I am not going to condone and enable with my endorsement every situation in which people enter debt. What I will state for the record is this: if you must agree to debt...

1) make certain the debt is necessary

2) make certain the debt is manageable

3) make certain the debt can be paid in an amount of time that is fair to all involved

If everyone who has ever assumed debt would have followed the previous criteria, not only would there be less outstanding debt in the world but less people would know the hardship of debt overall.

I have no doubt that many are in debt because of foolish decision-making. Many are in debt for no other reason than impulse; they saw it and had to have it. Many are in debt because of image and pride; desire to upkeep their image to run parallel with others who have luxurious amenities. This way of financially thinking and living will run someone so far in the ground that it may take a half-century to recover.

As a matter of fact, the longer I live the more difficult it is for me to discern who has money and who does not. Often, people who have the nicest luxuries and come across as the trendiest are immersed in debt. Often, those who look as if they have little to offer, that is, those who live modestly have more money than you would ever guess. Looks are not everything when it comes to money. Furthermore, we should not strive to spend money based on how luxuries will make us appear. This is pride in action. The irony here is this: the more shallow the spending habits...the deeper the debt.

When pride comes, then comes shame;

But with the humble is wisdom.

Proverbs 11:2

Pride goes before destruction,

And a haughty spirit before a fall.

Proverbs 16:18

A man's pride will bring him low,

But the humble in spirit will retain honor.

Proverbs 29:23

Here is a perfect example. The argument is do I buy it now and pay it back, or do I work now and pay as I go. The intangibles serve as the answer. Debt represents decisions you have made; the past. Cash represents the goals that you are striving to achieve; the future. I cannot place into words the difference between paying on something versus owning the same thing. I have been on both sides of the fence, so I can honestly address this issue. Whether it is a home, car, furniture, appliances, or etc., there is no comparison between financing and owning. I understand that it behooves some to rent a home or apartment because of maintenance or other extenuating circumstances. I am simply stating in general terms--from my experience—that there is much more satisfaction in owning than financing. The difference is in the feeling of satisfyingly owning something versus borrowing something. Again, those who choose to finance should enter their lease and loan agreements with the previous criteria in mind:

1) make certain the debt is necessary

2) make certain the debt is manageable

3) make certain the debt can be paid in an amount of time that is fair to all involved

I feel young as I write this book, so I feel I can address my following point accurately while shouldering some of the blame. Part of the problem with debt and the incorrect perception of debt is thanks my generation. I have seen a disturbing trend in young adults attempting to immediately gain everything that it took our parents a lifetime to achieve. Believe me, I am a great supporter of blessing the next generation and wanting more for the next generation than what the previous generation had, yet there are lessons to be learned along the way. There is the lesson of hard work. There is the lesson of discipline. There is the lesson of patience. There is the lesson of contentment. Also, there is the lesson of satisfaction, meaning it is a blessing to see something you want, whether a home, car, vacation, or whatever, set a goal, and then work hard to attain the desire of your heart. There is great satisfaction in working hard and achieving your goals. Contrary to some opinions, it is even greater satisfaction to work hard and achieve your dreams than to have your dreams handed to you.

Nothing is better for a man than that he should eat and drink, and that his soul should enjoy good in his labor. This also, I saw, was from the hand of God.

Ecclesiastes 2:24

There is a growing problem of people charging items with the intent of never fully paying for the items. People charge items at will, knowing they will never see the day when they own these items free and clear. This way of thinking is extremely foreign to me. If you need something so desperately that you would assume debt for it, I dare you to be desperate enough to work for it.

As you know, the purpose of this book is to bring to the forefront the spiritual decisions behind money. Therefore, and you guessed it, I am going to address the spiritual side of indebtedness, as well.

Take a few moments and analyze the reasons why you are in debt. I am not meaning to pile on you or conjure bad memories; however, if there is a behavioral deficiency, we need to address the problem at the root. Were you careless with your money? Did you make multiple or large purchases on impulse, pride, or maybe even out of lust? Is there a void of joy, peace, or contentment in your life, so much so that you attempted to fill the void with material objects?

If a behavioral problem or unhealthy lifestyle exists, your first step is to repent. God is ready and willingly to change your life for the better. The first step, however, is yours to make.

"As many as I love, I rebuke and chasten. Therefore be zealous and repent."

Revelation 3:19

Be encouraged: God can work with the humble, and He is ready to bring you on the road to recovery as only He can.

Create in me a clean heart, O God; and renew a right spirit within me.

Psalm 51:10 KJV

Do not stall. Do not beat around the bush: if you have sinned, repent. If you have been a careless, unwise steward of the resources God has given you, repent. I had to do it. I had to repent for poor financial decisions, but the sooner I made the situation right with God, the sooner I started on the road to recovery with my Heavenly Father holding my hand.

If we confess our sins, He is faithful and just to forgive us our sins and to cleanse us from all unrighteousness.

1 John 1:9

As you will find in the next chapter, admission and repentance are the first two steps on the road to recovery from debt.

Chapter Thirty-six

Debt: What Does God Think Continued: Seven Steps to Recovery from Debt

1) Admit that you have debt

Pull those hidden bills, invoices, and envelopes out of the drawers and cabinets of the abyss. As long as they remain in hiding, the situation will not improve; it will only worsen. Admission must take place. I have found that a main reason why people hide their debt is fear; the fear of knowing exactly how much they owe. Here is the key: when you handle your money by following the ways of God, you are no longer carrying the burden alone because God is with you. The situation might be difficult, and it might be a long road to travel; however, with God nothing is impossible. I ask you, does God live in fear? No. Therefore, as God walks with you, there is no reason for you to live in fear.

For God has not given us a spirit of fear, but of power and of love and of a sound mind.

2 Timothy 1:7

2) Repent to God...and ask forgiveness of the lender

This can be a hard pill to swallow, I know. However, let us not shirk our responsibility: If you have fallen in debt that you cannot pay or pay within the agreed time frame, you need to repent. Then, the next step is to ask forgiveness of those with whom you have entered the agreement; ask forgiveness of the lender. This takes humbleness. I realize the fear of rejection will be present as you humble yourself; however, the person or party on the other end of the agreement might show compassion on you. The compassion the other party displays might even be measured in dollars and cents. Unless you apologize, you will never know if the circumstances can be mitigated. If you explain to the other party about your situation, and I mean honestly explain and not try to deceive them, it might be a case in which they lessen the severity of the terms, lessen a portion of the overall debt, or cancel the debt completely. How will you know unless you humble yourself and ask? Like compassion, humbleness may save you dollars and cents, but pride will definitely cost you more.

"Agree with your adversary quickly, while you are on the way with him, lest your adversary deliver you to the judge, the judge hand you over to the officer, and you be thrown into prison. Assuredly, I say to you, you will by no means get out of there till you have paid the last penny."

Matthew 5:25, 26

The previous scripture is not meant to automatically label your lender as an obstinate adversary; rather, this scripture emphasizes the importance of fulfilling the vow you have made, that is, unless you are released from certain terms of the vow or the vow altogether.

Remember what we read earlier? We are snared by the words of our mouths, and it is better not to vow than to vow and not pay. If an agreement has been made, God expects us to embrace the agreement.

Maybe your debt is owed to a large, faceless corporation? I know there is this mentality of the little guys versus the big guys. Nevertheless, we are not solving this problem the world's way; we are solving it God's way. Own up to your debt, call the company, and see if a compromise can be reached. Accept responsibility for the agreement you made and ask God for His favor over the negotiations. Remember, if you are a child of God, He is with you.

3) Formulate a plan to repay your debt

God blesses planning. I know the debt facing you may seem impossible, but with God nothing is impossible. Furthermore, if you seek His wisdom to formulate a plan, I assure you, there is a plan to be found. God may even bring someone into your life or He may lay someone on your heart to help you formulate a plan. Either way, once you have sought the wisdom of God and a plan is on paper or on screen, God will bless the plan. Remember, draw near to God by drawing near to the ways of God, and God will draw near to you, meaning He will work the problem from His end.

Furthermore, while God is performing the supernatural on His end, be prepared to perform the natural and practical on your end. You may need to look at your expenses and let some things go. You may need to downsize your home. You may need to downsize to one car.

Eating-out may need to go. Cable may need to go. You may need to take a part-time job and devote your earnings toward debt (do not forget to bring God the tithe that belongs to Him). Some of these suggestions may seem shocking to you, but what you must know is as long as there are luxuries in your life that deter you from paying the debt you owe, God is not pleased. You need God to be pleased with you. You need God in your corner. You need to implement the ways of God to have any hope for financial freedom.

Remember:

"For which of you, intending to build a tower, does not sit down first and count the cost, whether he has enough to finish it—"

Luke 14:28

4) Start Paying Small Debts First (results are contagious)

I have had days at the office when there is so much to accomplish that I don't know where to start. Add the fact that some days I am less motivated than other days, and there is a huge problem on my hands. Here is a good practice: when I have much to do, I start with something small. If multiple projects are on my desk that individually require three hours, two hours, one hour, or fifteen minutes to complete, often times I will begin with the project that will take fifteen minutes. Results are contagious. I receive stamina and motivation from completing smaller projects, thus I am ready to tackle the larger projects next.

I view debt in the same way. If you have several debts to several people or companies confronting you, you must start somewhere. These debts will not resolve themselves. Isolate the smallest debt and focus your energy on paying that debt first. Two benefits will come from this: first, you will have one less debt to pay, and second, fear decreases as motivation increases. Next, move to the smallest remaining debt and continue the process. This will bring a sense of accomplishment. You will pay a debt and look around and say, "I'm still alive. I did it. Paying off this debt was not the end of me. Letting go a personal luxury to pay this debt was not the end of me. Making a sacrifice of time and money was not the end of me. Therefore, if I did it once with God's help, He and I can do it again."

"For who has despised the day of small things?"

Zechariah 4:10

This tactic of paying small debt first leads us perfectly to the next step.

5) Determine what you can pay toward debt and do not stop until all debts are paid

Once you pay the smallest debt, do not fall in the trap of taking that new-found amount of money and spending it elsewhere. Be committed to pay all debts until all debts are paid. Use momentum on your side; put a snowball-effect to work for you. Use that same amount of money toward your remaining debt, and as the debts begin to fall and extra money appears, re-direct that extra money toward your remaining debt, as well. Eventually, even the larger debts will begin to fall like dominos. Not to mention, while you are working the situation from your end, remember, God is working the situation from His end. I have never experienced an indebtedness plan taking as long as I initially anticipated once I began working the problem God's way.

Once you determine what you can pay toward debt, and once you begin knocking down individual debts one by one, you will become invigorated. You will look to apply even more of your money to pay other larger debts until nothing is standing except your cars and home. I encourage you: do not stop there! Do not be intimidated by the amount of your remaining debt. Do not listen to those who say it is impossible to own a home or pay cash for a home. I have had people tell me that paying cash for a home is impossible; all the while I sat across the table from them after paying for my home *in cash*. Continue to work the plan that has brought you this far. Begin to pay extra toward your cars and home. Shrink that five-year car loan in half. Shrink that thirty-year mortgage down to a third. Be diligent to the end.

He who has a slack hand becomes poor,

But the hand of the diligent makes rich.

Proverbs 10:4

6) Once all debts are paid, convert debt payments to savings

I realize my philosophy at this point will differ from the philosophies of others. I understand that it can take a significant amount of time to pay all debts, especially cars and homes, and that other needs arise in the meantime. Please read through my entire explanation before casting too much judgment, and, by the end, I will explain what I mean by converting debt payments into savings once all debts are paid.

I know what you are thinking. Once your debts are paid, you want me to give you permission to take a cruise and charge it, buy yourself something nice on credit, or ditch your budget along with the need to work diligently for the rest of your life. Well, not quite.

Please know: I believe it is important to reward yourself; even the one who reaps the harvest is entitled to enjoy the harvest. I have no problem with you spending within your means to celebrate the occasion of being free from debt. However, once your debts are paid, do not return to the person you were. Please do not scrap your financial plan and throw all caution to the wind just because you are debt free. Remember: if there had been a financial plan in the beginning, debt would not have become so overwhelming along the way.

Once that glorious day arrives and we remove all debt from atop our shoulders, the battle is not complete; we have simply dug ourselves from the pit beneath the battlefield. Now, it is time to do what we should have been doing all along: developing adequate savings in reserve.

The art of saving money by financial discretion is very biblical.

There is desirable treasure,

And oil in the dwelling of the wise,

But a foolish man squanders it.

Proverbs 21:20

A prudent man foresees evil and hides himself,

But the simple pass on and are punished

Proverbs 22:3

"Then that food shall be as a reserve for the land for the seven years of famine which shall be in the land of Egypt, that the land may not perish during the famine." So the advice was good in the eyes of Pharaoh and in the eyes of all his servants. And Pharaoh said to his servants, "Can we find such a one as this, a man (Joseph) in whom is the Spirit of God?"

Genesis 41:36-38

I think we would all agree that saving money is a good and noble premise. Even so, saving money comes easier for some than others, and I, admittedly, fall under the *others* category. As I referenced earlier, saving money has never been my strength. Therefore, my wife is in charge of that area of our financial planning. Even though savings is not an area in which I excel, I still recognize the importance of saving money. Here is the cold, hard truth. You may have the best financial plan in the world, and you may account for every predictable penny of income and every predictable penny of expense. There is only one problem: since when is life predictable?

Since when does life materialize exactly as we predict? I can document this fact only as it pertains to me: very rarely does a single day of my life materialize in the way I think it will. Life has a way of being more expensive than we ever think it will be. Unexpected, unpredictable costs litter this financial road on which we travel. Therefore, if we know this, if we have come to understand that uncertainty is a large part of life's profile, the responsibility to expect the unexpected becomes ours.

There is no magic wand to wave in the face of unexpected expenses to make them vanish. There is no avoiding the situation. As a matter of fact, the closest we can come to avoiding unexpected expenses is to brace for unexpected expenses. Do not get burned by the stove twice, thrice, or more. You need money in reserve. You need a cushion; a cushion to cushion the blow. You must build a plan to save money into your financial plan.

How many more times must we witness the truth to accept the truth? Life can be very unpredictable.

- Car repairs happen
- A/C repairs happen

- Furnace repairs happen
- Co-pays at the dentist office happen
- Birthday parties happen
- Unexpected travel to see an ill member of the family happens
- Worn-out clothes and shoes happen

How do we begin to predict what will happen from one day to the next? Furthermore, the unpredictability of life can get expensive. I encourage you: begin to incorporate saving money into your financial plan. Furthermore, do what I have done and enlist the help of someone if saving money is an area in which you struggle.

Believe me: I realize the challenges that come with trying to save money. I guarantee something unpredictable will arise and challenge the very purpose for your savings; something will try to drain your savings before you get the money saved. I guarantee you will save money for one area of life, and you will unexpectedly need to spend your savings on another area of life. I guarantee--at least once—you will feel as if you have been knocked to the ground as you watch your savings evaporate due to unpredictable hardships.

What is my advice to you when life is unpredictable? Be thankful that you have something in savings. Even if your savings gets wiped-out as soon as you save it, even if you have to use your savings for something other than what you originally intended, and even if you do not have enough in savings to cover all the unexpected cost, be thankful that you have something in savings. Be thankful that there is money in the account to be wiped-out. Be thankful that, even though you must unexpectedly spend it elsewhere, you have it in reserve. Something is better than nothing. Just think if nothing were in savings when life becomes unpredictable. Just think of how much more devastating the situation would be. Just think of how much further you would be in the hole. Start saving money and remind yourself that something is better than nothing.

Again, others will differ in philosophy from me on the topic of savings, and I am fine with that. Some believe that you must set a strict goal to save for a particular purpose and never touch that money for any other reason. As a matter of fact, I agree with this premise as long as your situation allows you to do so within reason. I don't want you to continually wipe-out the college fund you are building every other year, because, obviously, nothing will be there when you need it down the road. Nevertheless, as you are trying to develop a financial plan and get your feet under you, there might be instances when you have to take your savings and apply it where needed most. Sometimes we must put out fires with our savings, and I do not believe this is the end of the world. Our financial stability will improve in the future as we continue to apply our financial plan. Remember, always use discretion.

Eventually, our savings can be used for savings. Until then, we are doing what we have to do to get the situation under control. This is not a defeatist attitude; rather, I am predicting the unpredictability of life. I see saving money as a positive. I see saving money as a reason to encourage someone. I do not see saving money as a reason to reprimand someone when they must use their savings for a legitimate reason. Despite what you have been taught by me or by anyone else, here is what I am encouraging you to do: begin saving money. Get used to saving money. Get accustomed to saving money.

I recommend approaching the matter of saving money with much specificity. Using history as a guide, analyze and isolate those unexpected expenses that seem to manifest most frequently. You know by now that car repairs will happen. You may have multiple children in multiple sports leagues, and you know by now that the cost of entry fees and uniforms escalate each year. Should it be a surprise to any of us that Christmas comes once a year, and Christmas means Christmas gifts to purchase? How many people suffer a large financial setback each year because they unwisely take Christmas money from money meant for utilities? If you know enough people, someone has a birthday each week of the calendar year. Analyze and isolate those unexpected expenses that seem to manifest most frequently, and, when you do, you will notice something ironic: the more you analyze unexpected expenses...the less unexpected they will be. Hence, you will begin to expect these expenses. Hence, you will be ready for them as you cushion and brace for impact.

There is, of course, the question of how much money to save and for what purpose. Even when you are not saving for a specific purpose, you are still saving for a purpose; the purpose of the unexpected. I greatly recommend assigning every dollar you make for a specific purpose to prevent you from aimlessly spending. Nevertheless, begin by saving something, anything. Try saving one-hundred dollars per week, fifty dollars per week, twenty dollars per week, or etc. Again, begin by saving something. If all else fails, we should all be saving for retirement. I will not dole a large quantity of retirement options to you in this book (there are many people far more qualified than I am on this matter). Rather, I will simply let you know two facts regarding saving for retirement. First, pray and seek the wisdom of God regarding what retirement options to choose. Second, whatever retirement option you choose will require money to get started. So, as I wrote earlier, start saving something and start saving now.

My final thought on retirement is this. Some of you are probably my age or older, and you can easily remember what you were doing twenty years ago. I was in college, and it seems like yesterday. As quickly as those twenty years have passed, the next twenty will pass just as briskly, so start saving something and start saving now. Save something, save anything.

I realize some of you are looking at your financial plan/budget, of which I am most proud of you, and you do not see much remaining for savings once all necessary expenses are paid. Remember in a previous chapter how I presented examples of different financial plans, and I declared that no one financial plan/budget works for everyone? Keep that in mind as we proceed. We can be more creative when it comes to saving money than we think. Saving money includes not only saving what we have, but earning more money to save.

There are ways to earn money in smaller quantities to be saved for specific purposes. People are looking to pay someone for yard work. People are looking to pay someone to clean houses. Pizza restaurants are looking to pay someone to make deliveries. Department stores are looking for seasonal employees. These examples may not represent your dream job or career, but, if you need extra money, these examples are worth considering. Also, these small amounts can add up over time.

Please let me state the following for the record: I am not in favor of people overworking. I am not trying to take people from their loved ones for more hours each week. I understand many people feel stretched to the limit already regarding time. What I recommend is considering extra hours of work to earn extra money to be put for a specific purpose. I do not recommend getting more money simply for the sake of getting more money, and there is a difference.

Also, I recommend married couples and families working together toward a common goal of savings. For example, rather than a family going in debt every year to fund the family vacation, what if a family works together and assumes two neighborhood yards to upkeep each week? The family works together, the family bonds, and the money is set aside to fund the next family vacation. Just to assign some numbers to the discussion: taking care of two neighborhood yards each week at twenty-five dollars per yard for twenty-five weeks would amount to $1,250. This amount could, at the very least, make a dent in the next family vacation. Again, I am not promoting overworking people or stealing time from them and their families; however, if your family spends three, four, or five nights at home on the couch watching television per week, then at least one of those evenings can be better spent earning money to save money.

Maybe it is a case where a family cannot work in the same place at the same time. As an alternative, what if the family devotes one four-hour block each week to individually earning money for the next family trip. What if dad mows a neighborhood yard while mom cleans a small house while one teenager babysits while the other teenager delivers pizzas? What if everyone donates their proceeds to the family-trip savings fund? If the tithe is brought from the proceeds and a firstfruits offering is given above the tithe, the first part of the family project will be blessed as well as the end of the family project. Don't be surprised if the family finishes sooner or above the targeted-goal when all is said and done.

The family-trip example is one of many. The point is sometimes we must get creative to save money, and one way to be creative in saving money is earning more money to save.

Here is the good news: saving money can be habit forming. The more you save...the more you become accustomed to saving, and the more natural you will feel when doing it. I encourage you to weather the early storms and hardships of trying to save money. The satisfaction of having money when you need it will be worth it in the end.

Regarding the concept of saving money, there is one more item I must address. Yes, most of the time I list *savings* behind *paying debt* on my list of financial priorities, and here is why. It is a great habit to start saving money today. However, there is another factor to consider. If you have debt that continues to accumulate interest at an accelerate clip, as long as this debt goes unpaid and unchecked, any savings you set aside can easily be consumed by this same interest. Therefore, as you formulate your financial plan with God's help, you must use discretion in weighing which option to emphasize: paying debt or saving money. I believe it is wise to have an emergency savings fund, and as I have written several times, start saving something, anything. Still, it is essential to get debt paid down and paid off. Furthermore, saving money for a vacation is not a wise while interest-accumulating debt continues to knock at the door. Yes, save money; however, use discretion while absolutely keeping debt at the forefront of your mind until all debt is gone.

7) Trust and Serve God

Yes, the thought of debt is overwhelming; even the strategies to get out of debt can be overwhelming. As you consider all the factors, such as income, expense, tithes, offerings, debt, savings, unexpected expenses, and etc., rather than get submerged in a haze of detail, I want you to keep your goal as simple and pure as possible. Just remember to trust and serve God. Our anchor through all the planning, managing, obtaining, and distribution of money is to trust and serve God.

Trust and serve God as you climb to a new financial level. Trust and serve God when you feel as if setbacks kick you to a lower level. Trust and serve God when things begin to change. Trust and serve God when it feels like things will never change. Trust and serve God when the bottom line looks great. Trust and serve God when there is more month than money.

God is your constant through every episode, encounter, and season. Life will change; God will not. Hold to God through every trial and rejoice with God in every triumph. Let us, in fact, just settle the situation in our hearts right now: we will trust and serve God. Let's pray.

Father, in the name of Jesus, we humbly approach you, and I agree with my brothers and sisters that no amount of financial debt can overshadow the debt of sin. When you sent Jesus, sin was defeated. Therefore, if you can defeat the greatest debt, what is this financial debt in your eyes other than an opportunity to show your great glory? Give us your wisdom, give us your discipline, and give us the desired result. Become everything to these precious people. I stand with them on this side of the mountain, and I pre-celebrate with them on the other side of the mountain...because THIS MOUNTAIN IS GOING DOWN! Thank you for doing it, God, in the name of Jesus. So be it.

Chapter Thirty-seven

My Story Continued: Mistakes and Forgiveness...Again

The next phase of my story goes hand in hand with the book you are reading today. I can remember a desire to write at the age of ten. I believe that is how God works. He bestows gifts to us at birth; even before birth—at conception. He forms us in the wombs of our mothers, and before He forms us He knows us, meaning He knows what He intends to do with our lives even before we arrive on the scene. God has that much forethought and foreknowledge pertaining to your life. He has great plans for you. Furthermore, not only does God impart gifts to us, He is so good that He grants us an inherent, innate desire to fulfil our gifts, which, again, is why I could discern a desire to write at a young age. Teachers and other classmates could discern this desire, as well. Teachers would comment on my gift and other kids would push to hear my stories read aloud in class. I am not boasting. Rather, I give all glory to God because He is the One who grants the gift.

However, I grossly erred in the next phase of my life: I fell in love with the gift above the One who gives the gift. I began to fall in love with the resource while neglecting the source. I became zealous to write books in my late-twenties. I knew God had called me to write, and nothing was going to prevent me from writing. I became consumed with finishing my first book to the point where I was not at peace until it was finished. I convinced myself life would be better once I finished my first book. I had no doubt there would be both accolades and financial benefits. It is true: I still wanted to point people to Jesus. Even so, in the midst of my zeal, my well-intentioned zeal, I got caught up in the moment, and my desire got the best of me.

I finished my first book and there was a great sense of relief. However, something happened that I never anticipated. What happened? Nothing happened. My first book--though well-received with many encouraging testimonials—didn't saturate the marketplace like I thought it would. I was certain the book would transform countless lives while shooting to the pinnacle of the best-sellers' lists. The book certainly made a great impact but only on a small level. Disappointed but not quenched, my zeal persisted. My desire to write my first book was soon bested by my desire to write my second book. I wrote a third book, and I was certain my footing as a legitimate author would be solidified by publishing multiple books. Again, despite great feedback, and despite the fact that I was and still am extremely proud of each of my books, none of my first three books made an impact like I had intensely hoped.

This is where I admittedly made a colossal mistake. Furthermore, this mistake would not only affect me, but it would affect my wife and children because my family is attached to every decision I make as a husband and father. Focused on numbers, aggrandized numbers, I refused to settle for anything less than a powerful impact.

Instead of seeking God for what He would have me to do next, I tried to implement a forced resurrection on my books. Rather than move forward, I looked back, and I pumped more and more money into my previous books. I generated more copies and generated more advertising. I had always been the guy who stayed away from debt. Debt, of course, was what I avoided at all cost and encouraged others to do the same. I was the guy, in fact, who had staved off the most enormous debt of all: the thirty-year mortgage. Yet, here I was, ready to go back on every principle that had gotten me to this point in life. All of this, just to push my books into a marketplace where they were not wanted, just to offer more supply where there was no demand.

Yes, I went into debt to promote my books, and this decision entangled me, my wife, and our children with debt for the next seven years. It was not an enormous debt; however, it was unwarranted debt, and it did change our lives. Looking back, I am convinced that it was not God's will for me to ensnare us with such a yolk of bondage. This debt had a long-reaching, over-arching impact on countless decisions in our lives. This debt affected whether we could go on vacation or not, whether we could buy certain furniture or not, whether we could buy certain clothes or not, whether we could go out for certain dinners or not, and whether we could go out for entertainment or not. This debt even caused us to put necessary home repairs on hold. It seemed unfair, but one decision, one hasty decision in one moment in time rippled pervasively and touched every area of our lives. As a result, we would have to say *no* many times over the next several years because of my decision; *no* to us and *no* to our children. It hurts me to admit it, but I cost my family many blessings: moments of joy, moments of laughter, moments of peace, and etc. Again, I accept the fact that my decisions as husband and father--as head of my household—negatively impacted our family.

But, God is good, God is faithful, and God is merciful. My wife and I committed to no longer live in debt. I admitted my mistake, and then I apologized to my wife and repented to God for entering debt when He had already set me free. Once we did this, once we made the commitment, God set our feet on the path to deliverance again. We continued to do everything we knew to do. We lived for God, we brought our tithe to the house of the Lord, we gave offerings above our tithe, we blessed others, and we blessed the Nation of Israel; God's chosen people.

Furthermore, I began to do something else, and had I not gone through my experience, I never would have learned the following lesson. So, again, God is good.

Since the Word of God is true, if a true statement is made, we will be able to trace that statement back to the Bible. Even if an expression is a paraphrasing, if the essence of the paraphrasing is true, we will still be able to trace it back to the Bible.

Every word of God is pure;

He is a shield to those who put their trust in Him.

Proverbs 30:5

I began to apply a principle that I learned along the way from a business acquaintance. This person shared with me: if you want to make your dreams come true, make someone else's dream come true first. I thought about it, and this statement is true, and this statement is biblical.

“Give (not just your money, but your time, effort and concern) and it will be given to you: good measure, pressed down, shaken together, and running over will be put into your bosom. For with the same measure that you use (your desire to see the dreams of others come true), it will be measured back to you (your dreams will come true).”

Luke 6:38 (my emphasis added)

Do not be deceived, God is not mocked; for whatever a man sows, that he will also reap. For he who sows to his flesh will of the flesh reap corruption, but he who sows to the Spirit will of the Spirit reap everlasting life. And let us not grow weary in well doing, for in due season we shall reap if we do not lose heart. Therefore, as we have opportunity, let us do good to all, especially to those who are of the household of faith.

Galatians 6:7-10

“Therefore, whatever you want men to do to you, do also to them, for this is the Law and the Prophets.”

Matthew 7:12

I began to do things for other people without expecting anything in return. I was not giving to get. Instead, I was giving to give. Case in point: I knew someone who was trying to get an idea off the ground. So, knowing full well what it's like to try to get an idea off the ground, I began to give that person's goal some of my time each day for a certain number of days each week. When the person's idea eventually got off the ground, the person was so thankful for what I had done that the person rewarded me financially. Again, I did not give of myself and my time to get anything in return; rather, I gave just to give, and, as a result, I reaped.

My wife and I in the meantime continued our commitment to getting out of debt, and as we continued to live for God and do what was possible within our abilities, God expedited the process for us to get out of debt. We did what was possible, and God did what was impossible. Blessings started appearing from all over the place. Believe me, several obstacles manifested as we made a concerted effort to get out of debt. The need for car repairs would surface along with other unexpected expenses, and there were many temptations to fold and give up. However, in response to the obstacles, something would always seem to happen to offset these hurdles. Without us asking anyone, people would suddenly offer to pay for a car repair or bless us with money…just because. It got to the point where we could see a light at the end of the tunnel.

With the finish line in sight, we bore down, and, oh man, did we bear down. I remember a particular two-week stretch in which we slashed our food budget to the point where we were simply making sure the kids had enough to eat. My wife and I, on the other hand, threw together whatever we could. Obviously, eating out was not an option. We even organized our trips with the car to allow us as few trips as possible to save on gas. Seemingly everything was put on hold for that two-week time frame, but, with God's help and by His grace, we did it. Yes, we paid off our final piece of debt. All thanks to God, we were debt free again, and we are still debt free today.

When I look back on the road to freedom from debt that God allowed me to walk, here is my final snapshot. I started giving to God and believing for a debt-free home in my mid-to-late twenties, and by the age of forty-one I had not only escaped debt once...but twice. Most people will tell you that it will take thirty years before you can pay off your home and be debt free. I am here to state that by using the blueprint, the Word of God, I got out of debt twice in fifteen years, which, obviously, is half of thirty. So, instead of becoming free from debt once in thirty years, I became debt free twice in half the time. Again, if God can bring me out of debt twice, He can surely bring you out of debt once. I might not be a millionaire, but I'm debt free.

Chapter Thirty-eight

The Saddest Story: Quitting on Your Harvest before the Time

I have written at great length about sowing seed by faith throughout this book. Ironically, sowing seed is not the most difficult part of trusting God financially. I believe many people find the courage to initially trust God and sow their seed. Obviously, reaping the harvest is pure elation. Therefore, if sowing seed is not the most difficult part of trusting God, and if we all know that reaping the harvest is joyful, the question is during what part of the process do most people fall short? The answer: many people quit on their harvest before the time.

Continuing to trust God after you have sown seed and before you see the harvest is crunch-time. This is where you earn your stripes, where the rubber meets the road, or insert your clichéd expression of choice here. Trusting God during the maturation process of the harvest is the most difficult test. Why? This is why: you have sown the seed, you made the effort, you made the sacrifice, and now you are waiting. The last time I checked, waiting is not something most people enjoy doing. I will admit that waiting is not atop my list of pleasantries. Waiting takes patience. Patience is in direct conflict with the desire of the flesh. We want what we want, and we want it now.

When you first sow seed after finding good soil, there is excitement (we should be excited because, remember, God loves a cheerful giver). You give to God or you give to bless others, and the sensation is refreshing. You helped. You made a difference. You made the sacrifice. You exercised your faith in God. Then time passes...and more time passes... and more time passes...and suddenly that initial surge of enthusiasm wanes cool. You were obedient, and you gave to someone in need. In the meantime, you are facing your own financial crunch. Who is going to help you? You helped others? Where is the love offering when you need it? Where is the wheelbarrow full of money? Where is the dump truck full of money backing up to your house? You sowed...but when will you reap?

This is the crucial moment. You have done the right thing. You have sown seed. You are expecting a harvest and in the meantime...nothing. This is where people surrender, throw in the towel, and quit on their harvest before the time. They begin to speak doubt. They begin to complain. They lack contentment, and the little contentment they have becomes less and less. They begin to lack appreciation regarding their relationship with God. They forget that God has brought them from a long way, and He will never leave them nor forsake them. Some of them even turn from serving God altogether from the disappointment they are feeling.

I am not casting judgment: I have felt this way, as well. I sowed seed, I did what the Bible taught, I had faith, and then...nothing. Days passed, weeks passed, months passed, even years passed, and I became doubtful; not only doubtful but angry. "Why would God have me sow seed if He was not going to bring the harvest," I asked myself...and Him. My frustration grew. I said words and took actions that were embarrassing. I said words and took actions that were embarrassing in front of my wife and my children. I, in fact, was acting like a child. I did not get what I wanted when I wanted it, so I pouted. I complained. I murmured. Suddenly, the times when I had instructed my children not to complain came to my memory. What a hypocrite. I was acting the very same way.

Then, I began to read the Bible.

My brethren, count it all joy when you fall into various trials, knowing that the testing of your faith produces patience. But let patience have its perfect work, that you may be perfect and complete, lacking nothing.

James 1:2-4

And let us not be weary in well doing: for in due season we shall reap, if we faint not.

Galatians 6:9 KJV

Blessed is the man

Who walks not in the counsel of the ungodly,

Nor stands in the path of sinners,

Nor sits in the seat of the scornful;

But his delight is in the law of the Lord;

And in His law he meditates day and night.

He shall be like a tree

Planted by the rivers of water,

That brings forth its fruit in its season,

Whose leaf also shall not wither;

And whatever he does shall prosper.

Psalm 1:1-3

But those who wait on the Lord

Shall renew their strength;

They shall mount up with wings like eagles,

They shall run and not be weary,

They shall walk and not faint.

Isaiah 40:31

Then, I began to take inventory of the good gifts in my life: the air I breath; the unparalleled blueness of the sky; the ground on which I stand; the trees that give me shade; the water that flows through the hills; the loved ones God has placed in my life; a mother and father who, if nothing else, brought me into this world and gave me an opportunity to know Jesus; my spouse; my children; my friends; the roof over my head; the shirt on my back; the shoes on my feet; and the list is endless.

The truth is this: future contentment does not exist. You are either content now or you will never be content. It is illogical to decree that you will be content based on a future contingency or occurrence. Contentment can only be settled in the present tense. You either settle contentment with God in your heart today…or who knows what tomorrow will hold?

What an opportunity to settle *all* issues with God. He stands and waits, He is in position, and He is ready to hear you call His name. Jesus died for this very moment. Jesus bore sin and shame to keep you from carrying your current load. What a savior. Release your faith in God. Ask for a new beginning. Even if you asked once and have fallen short, we have all fallen short of the glory of God. Ask forgiveness of your sins. Ask Jesus to cleanse your heart with His supernatural blood. Ask God to empower you with His wonderful Holy Spirit that you may live pleasing to Him each day. Even if you have given your heart to God in the past, return to Him in a fresh way today. Remember the words of Jesus,

"Come to Me, all you who labor and are heavy laden, and I will give you rest."

Matthew 11:28

When the presence of God resides in your heart, waiting for the harvest is not such trouble after all. Why should it be? When you have Jesus, you have everything you will ever need.

Chapter Thirty-nine

The Promise of Financial Prosperity Is for Everyone

I, in this brief chapter, will generate great hope and, at the same time, great disappointment.

I enjoy good news, so let us start there: the promise of financial prosperity is for everyone, regardless of income, family status, educational status, race, man or woman; it does not matter. The promise of financial prosperity is for everyone because the promises of God are for everyone willing to receive.

For all the promises of God in Him are Yes, and in Him Amen, to the glory of God through us.

2 Corinthians 1:20

The promises of God are designed to come to pass in our lives to glorify Him. When we glorify God, we will desire to bless others, as well. God desires to be glorified in our lives, not only in one area of our lives but in every area of our lives. God desires for us to be a blessing to others, not only in one area of our lives but in every area of our lives.

Beloved, I pray that you may prosper in all things and be in health, just as your soul prospers.

3 John, verse 2

God is a good God. Salvation is for all mankind. God sent Jesus for everyone. This is a promise of God: that whoever will call on the name of the Lord will be saved. As a matter of fact, all the promises of God are for everyone who will receive: salvation; physical healing; emotional, mental, and spiritual healing; restoration of relationships; and, yes, financial prosperity.

God provides a clean slate for all who enter the world. We are all born with potential, promise, and possibility. We are all born with the purpose to have a relationship with God. Even those born with special needs, mentally and physically, have been born with the purpose to have a relationship with God. Our lives are blank canvasses at birth, and the picture we paint--better yet, the picture we allow or don't allow God to paint through us—will yield a final result and depiction at the end of our days.

We are given the ability to work, labor, dream, push, strive, create, innovate, persist, and persevere. We are all granted gifts and callings from God. God institutes abilities within us to be cultivated as we grow. God desires for us to use these gifts to glorify Him and bless others. Since God calls us, He equips us; that is if we are willing to walk through whichever open door He desires through each season of our lives. Even when life is difficult, and I assure you that life will be very difficult, God still balances the difficult times with His grace and presence.

And He said to me, "My grace is sufficient for you, for My strength is made perfect in weakness." Therefore most gladly I will rather boast in my infirmities, that the power of Christ may rest upon me.

2 Corinthians 12:9

It is the desire of God for all of us to be His children, and it is the desire of God for all of His children to prosper.

Here is news that might be disappointing to some. God will cause His children to prosper financially regardless of what they do for a living. Regardless of their job, career, education, or vocation, God will cause His children to prosper. It is simply the responsibility of the children of God to learn and apply the principles of the Word of God to their money. If the children of God apply the financial principles of the Word of God, they will prosper. Once you enter the Kingdom of God, God is an equal-opportunity employer.

This news might be disappointing to you if you are well-educated, yet you have never entered the kingdom of God. This news might be disappointing to you if you were born into a wealthy family, yet you have never entered the kingdom of God. This news might be disappointing to you if you have a distinguished career by the hard labor of your own hands.

Possibly you spent countless hours studying in the halls of a prestigious university, countless hours applying yourself in law school, or countless hours persevering through medical school. Possibly you feel as if you deserve financial prosperity more than those who have not travelled the same road or put in the same time.

This is the truth: God will prosper who He desires to prosper. Furthermore, if there are two groups of people in this world, His children and those who are not His children, which group will He prosper in your opinion? Yes, the children God have the advantage of knowing God, living in a relationship with God, praying to God, reading the Word of God, and, if they apply the ways of God to their money, the children of God have the advantage of prospering more than those who are not His children.

Remember, I am fully aware that people who are not children of God prosper in this world. I realize there is a world financial system at work, and the temptation exists for all of us to yield to this system to get ahead. I understand this world financial system is based more on what we can see as opposed to faith. I understand the monetary value that we can touch is more immediately satisfying than things of faith. However, the difference is this: the monetary, tangible riches of this world only satisfy for a season, but those riches that manifest by faith will endure.

I am very thankful for those who have profitable careers, those who come from wealthy families, and those who have worked diligently to arrive at a prominent place of stature. We need these people to be generous people. We need their expertise. We need them to share with others the right way to success (if indeed they have chosen the right way to success).

However, the ultimate combination of prosperity is when children of God apply themselves and achieve great accomplishments in the world in which we live. We need children of God who are well-educated. We need children of God who come from wealthy families. We need children of God who will apply themselves and perform the diligent work necessary to pass through open doors that God has set before them. It is the desire of God for all of us to be His children, and it is the desire of God to bless His children.

I am drawing this book to a close, and I desire to leave you with the following. Only God knows the calling He has for your life. Only God knows in fullness the road you are meant to travel and the open doors along the way. Only God knows what tomorrow holds. Therefore, God is the only One worth seeking. Once we seek Him, His will for us can be found and applied, and the benefits are endless; including financial prosperity.

Therefore, if God calls you to go to college, then go to college. If God calls you to be a stay-at-home wife and mother (which is the most difficult job on the planet), then stay at home and raise a family. If God calls you to be a pastor, then be a pastor. If God calls you to be an auto mechanic, then be an auto mechanic. If God calls you to be a missionary on the other side of the world, then be a missionary. If God calls you to be an accountant, then be an accountant. Be whatever God calls you to be.

I know the next logical question that comes to mind: if God desires for us to prosper financially more than anyone else, how can auto mechanics, missionaries, or stay-at-home moms prosper more than others? Not all of us are called to be doctors, lawyers, and college professors. What of the rest of us? Should we try to wedge and pry our way into a calling that God has not called us to fulfill?

Absolutely not! Look at me. I am your proof. You will find many people much more qualified in selected areas of life than I am, and yet here I am: I am not a millionaire, but I'm debt free. Therefore, taking into the consideration the goodness and equality of God, we arrive at the following conclusion: if we apply the financial principles of the Word of God to earn, manage, and invest money, we are thus eligible to prosper financially in whichever calling God has for us to fulfill. Remember our chapters on sowing and reaping? We come to the ultimate conclusion that if we give we will receive. Here is the key: receive Jesus, find the calling God has for you, apply the financial principles of the Word of God to the area of your money (just as you would any other area) and be blessed.

Yes, the promise of financial prosperity is for everyone.

Please read the following words of Jesus, and I will explain to you a deeper meaning of this scripture that I have come to understand.

"No one can serve two masters; for either he will hate the one and love the other, or else he will be loyal to the one and despise the other. You cannot serve God and mammon."

Matthew 6:24

The obvious explanation of this scripture is that we must make a decision: will God be the God of our lives, or will we serve money (mammon refers to treasure, especially when it is opposed to God); we cannot serve both. There will be times in your life when you will inevitably need to make a decision to either pursue money at all costs or preserve your faith in the righteous ways of God. All of us, in short, have been tempted to steal for personal gain. What we do at that moment of temptation reflects our ultimate loyalty. Do we serve God or do we serve money?

Here is a deeper meaning to this scripture. Many of us desire to do good and wonderful things for God and others? We desire to start a foundation, or a ministry, or a non-profit corporation, possibly feeding and clothing others; however, we are not able to act on these good and wonderful desires. Why are we not able to act? Money.

Sometimes it is not a lack of desire or knowledge, or sometimes it is not even opposition from others that keeps us from fulfilling these desires. Rather, it is a lack of money that keeps us from fulfilling the God-given desires of our hearts. I have been at this point, and let me state it for the record: it is one of the most frustrating experiences in life.

We cannot serve two masters to accomplish what God desires for us to fully accomplish. We cannot serve vision and serve lack at the same time. We cannot serve growth and serve malnourishment at the same time. We cannot serve prosperity and serve poverty at the same time. When I reference serving vision, growth, and prosperity, of course, I am not declaring that we serve these ideas; instead, we serve a God who desires to bring vision, growth, and prosperity. In short, don't serve money because you want to serve money, and don't serve money because you have to serve money.

The road to prosperity is to enter a relationship with God through Jesus Christ. The road to prosperity is to apply the Word of God and ways of God to our lives. The road to prosperity is to apply the Word of God and ways of God to every area of our lives; salvation, healing, relationships, and, yes, money. Why would God exclude a single area of our lives from the equation? He would not.

Beloved, I pray that you may prosper in all things and be in health, just as your soul prospers.

3 John, verse 2

God desires to bless you that you may be a blessing to others. God is glorified through your life and others are blessed. Whatever God has called you to do...do it and be blessed. You can know every good accomplishment in the lot of life that God has given you.

May the Lord Jesus Christ be your salvation today, may He be your healing, may He restore your relationships, and may He cause you to prosper in every area of your life. More than anything, through you, may God be glorified and others blessed. You are blessed to be a blessing. Make the spiritual decision to follow God today...and see the physical results come to pass. Don't serve money because you want to serve money, and don't serve money because you have to serve money.

Chapter Forty

The Place Where Possible Meets Impossible

Pretty much everyone wants to see the impossible come to pass. However, you cannot cross the threshold of the impossible until you have first traveled across the entire region of what is possible, covering the entire distance. I live in the Midwest. You cannot cross from Illinois into Kansas until you have travelled completely across Missouri. You cannot cross into Canada or Mexico until you have travelled completely across the United States. You cannot step into the Atlantic or Pacific Oceans until you have completely traveled to the East or West coasts. Sure, you can try to find ways to go around the clear and obvious way. However, your travel time will be indefinitely delayed, and so will your harvest.

Many times we err, only completing fifty percent of the journey, only completing fifty percent of what is possible for us to accomplish. Sometimes we may cover seventy-five percent or even ninety percent of the journey. However, until we accomplish everything that God has made possible for us to accomplish, we are not yet ready to cross into the land, the region, the territory of the impossible. Furthermore, we are not ready, and we are not deserved. How can we expect to be entrusted with what is impossible if we can't responsibly manage what is possible?

Jesus said,

"He who is faithful in what is least is faithful also in much; and he who is unjust in what is least is unjust also in much."

Luke 16:10

What is possible for us to accomplish from a financial standpoint? It is possible for us to bring the tithe to God. It is possible for us to give offerings above the tithe. It is possible for us to construct a budget (a plan). It is possible for us to restrain spending to pay our debts. It is possible for us to harness spending to save money. It is possible for us to work five hours of overtime when afforded us. It is possible for us to shop for clothes at a thrift store if need be. It is possible for us to operate out of humbleness rather than fear or pride. It is possible for us to buy groceries that are not name-brand and etc. They might hurt, they might stretch us, but none of these sacrifices are going to kill anyone. Furthermore, all of these sacrifices are within our scope of ability, within the scope of what is possible. How can we ask God to perform the impossible when we refuse to perform what is possible?

I can remember specific times in my life—more than one—when I prayed to God to deliver me from a situation, whether it was a task or a commitment. I not only remember praying to Him about these situations, but I also remember His answer: "Finish what you started." In other words, I was to finish what God called me to finish. If I would finish what I could, He would do the rest.

Honestly, that was not the answer I desired in return. However, in retrospect, what was God doing? God was mandating for me to travel the complete region of what was possible before I could cross the threshold of what was impossible, which brings me to an astounding revelation from my relationship with God. It hit me one day! It was a *moment,* an epiphany. The light switched on. My heart, soul, mind, and spirit all booted up. All of those years serving God and suddenly there it was.

God has never once asked me to do the impossible. Think about that and let it sink in. When has God ever called me to do the impossible? How could He? Why would He? God knows fully well that I can't do the impossible because if I could do the impossible then whatever is impossible would no longer be impossible to me. Got it?

Let's try it like this. I cannot save myself from sin. However, I can repent and ask Jesus to save me from sin. The saving from sin is impossible to me, but repenting and asking Jesus to save me is possible to me. Once I repent and acknowledge the need for a savior, it is the equivalent of travelling across the entire territory of what is possible. Now, having travelled that entire region, after doing what was expected and possible for me to accomplish, I am ready to cross the threshold of the impossible. This is where I leave off and God picks up.

On the topic of money, you cannot cause someone to forgive a loan. This is impossible to you. However, you can bring your tithes, bring your offerings, believe, pray, and fast. Once you do what is possible for you to do, once you put forth the effort and seriously apply your faith in God and in His Word, God is the only One who can take your situation and do something with it from there. If you will begin a serious approach to extricating yourself from debt by doing what is possible, by spending less on luxuries and applying extra money to pay down your debt more quickly, God will cause the back end of your debt to supernaturally dwindle in a way that only He can accomplish. You do what is possible and let God handle what is impossible.

So, let's get to it. What is possible for you to do that you have not been doing? I have mentioned a litany of ideas in this book on cutting costs and saving money. Again, I am not encouraging you to overwork and neglect your family. Conversely, I am not encouraging you to go hungry or cause your children to go hungry. Instead, I am encouraging you to roll up your sleeves and start earning more where you can earn more and spend less where you can spend less. I am encouraging you to travel across the entire region of what is possible, and this will ensure that you make it to the threshold of the impossible. This is where you leave off and God picks up.

I mean zero disrespect to the Government of the United States with my following comment. In fact, I thank God for America, and I wouldn't trade America for any other country in the world. Let it be known that before any entitlement plans of the U.S. were ever set forth and rolled into action, the Word of God was, is, and always will be.

For even when we were with you, we commanded you this: If anyone will not work, neither shall he eat.

2 Thessalonians 3:10

When It comes to traveling across the region of what is possible, the first step many need to take is to go to work, to labor, to get a job. God can only bless and multiply what you give Him, and if there is nothing coming in, then there is nothing to bless and multiply. You can pray for a large harvest of multiplication all you want, but remember: zero times any number is still zero.

Now, let's be truthful! You know I'm not referencing those who can't physically work or those who are trying but can't get a job, so don't even play that game. Instead, I am underscoring the difference between those who can't work and those who won't work, and there is a difference. If you are able to work but refuse to work, you have made it as far as you will ever make it. If you simply milk the system for handouts, all the while you could do more, be advised that you have gone as far as you will ever go in life. This is it! Look around: you have reached your potential. Furthermore, don't make excuses, don't blame anyone else, and don't be jealous of what anyone else has. God is an equal opportunity employer and supplier, and if you are willing to work and willing to ask God to provide a job for you, the last time I checked, He will do it.

"For with God nothing will be impossible."

Luke 1:37

Again, do you need proof that God can do the impossible? I am your proof. I am a man of average height, average build, and, according to standardized testing, average intelligence. I am your proof; just a regular guy...with regular grades in school...from a regular city in the Midwest, raised in a regular family of hardworking people. If God can do it through me, He can do it through anybody.

I encourage you: start making a list of what to do first, a list of how to begin travelling across the region of what is possible. First and foremost, I encourage you to ask God what He would have you to do.

If any you lacks wisdom, let him ask of God, who gives to all liberally and without reproach, and it will be given to him.

James 1:5

Spend time before the Lord, ask Him for wisdom, and go from there. He will help you formulate a plan to accomplish what is possible. Then, praise God, He will be there to take over when you are ready to cross from what is possible to what is impossible.

Again, always remember:

"For with God nothing will be impossible."

Luke 1:37

My final words to you are these: if you ask me for my opinion, I believe you are going to do it! I believe the impossible will happen for you because you are going to do what it is possible. I believe a true-life account of deliverance is ready to spring from within you; a testimony. I am conversing with future debt-free men and women right now. Furthermore, because I believe you are going to do what is possible, and because I fully know God will do what is impossible, it is only a matter of time. That's it: it is only a matter of time. I look forward to the day when you say the words, "I'm not a millionaire, but I'm debt free."